Walk Herri

written by
Stuart W. Greig

1st Edition: January 2010, this 4th Edition: September 2019

published by
Pocket Routes
www.pocketroutes.co.uk

ISBN: 978-1916117709

Copyright © 2019 by Stuart W. Greig

All rights reserved. No part of this publication may be reproduced, distributed, or transmitted in any form or by any means, including photocopying, printing, recording, or other electronic or mechanical methods, without the prior written permission of the author, except in the case of brief quotations embodied in critical reviews and certain other non-commercial uses permitted by copyright law. For permission requests, or to enquire about distribution options or reprint fees, contact **stuart@pocketroutes.co.uk**

Front cover:
Stone barn above Keld, Swaledale

Other Titles from the Author

Published by Pocket Routes
www.pocketroutes.co.uk

Tributaries Walk: An 8-day, 93-mile circular walk discovering the best rivers, valleys and high paths in the Yorkshire Dales (ISBN: 978-1916117716)

The Rivers Trilogy: three walks following iconic English rivers

Swale Way: A 6-day, 80-mile walk beside the Swale from its end near Boroughbridge, to its source in Swaledale (ISBN: 978-1788089029)

Yoredale Way: A 6-day, 73-mile walk following the Ure, from its source, through Wensleydale to Boroughbridge, near its end (ISBN: 978-1916117723)

Eden Way: A 6-day, 88-mile walk following the Eden from the Solway to its source, high in the fells of the Yorkshire Dales (ISBN: 978-1916117730)

Published by Trailblazer Publications
www.trailblazer-guides.com

Pennine Way 2019 (5th Edition): Britain's first National Trail, running for 256 miles from Edale in the Peak District to Kirk Yetholm in the Scottish Borders (ISBN: 978-1912716029)

Walking the Herriot Way

You can order a pin badge from the website
www.herriotway.com

DEDICATION

The freedom I have, to walk the hills and valleys of this wonderful country, is only possible through the support of my wife Christine, without whom I would be forever lost.

CONTENTS

PART 1 - PLANNING	………… ………… …………	1
INTRODUCTION …………	………… ………… …………	2
GETTING TO AND FROM	………… ………… …………	9
WHEN TO WALK	………… ………… …………	13
GENERAL WALKING ADVICE	………… …………	17
KIT ………… ………… …………	………… …………	23
HOSTELS & B&BS	………… ………… …………	26
CAMPING ………… …………	………… …………	30
SUPPORT SERVICES	………… ………… …………	34
NAVIGATION ………… …………	………… …………	38
WATERFALLS OF THE HERRIOT WAY	…………	40
HERRIOT WAY WEBSITE …………	………… …………	44
PART 2 - ROUTE DESCRIPTION	………… …………	45
SECTION 1 - AYSGARTH TO HAWES	………… …………	46
SECTION 2 - HAWES TO KELD	………… …………	65
SECTION 3 - KELD TO REETH (HIGH)	…………	79
SECTION 3 - KELD TO REETH (LOW)	…………	91
SECTION 4 - REETH TO AYSGARTH	…………	103
PART 3 - THE MAPS	………… ………… …………	117
OVERVIEW MAP …………	………… ………… …………	118

Walking the Herriot Way

PART 1 - PLANNING

"The peace which I always found in the silence and emptiness of the moors filled me utterly."

James Herriot

INTRODUCTION

WHAT IS IT?
It would be difficult to describe a route that more fairly represents the joys of walking in the Yorkshire Dales, than the Herriot Way.

Along its 52-mile (84 km) length you visit beautiful valleys, high, open fells and rolling, heather-clad moorland. You cross one of the highest points in Yorkshire, visit historic monuments and pass through a barren industrial wilderness; laid bare through lead mining. Anyone walking the Herriot Way will have had a fantastic introduction to the Yorkshire Dales.

The walk is named after James Herriot; the fictional name given to the real-life veterinary surgeon who lived and worked in the Dales for many years. In life James Herriot was really Alf Wight and the origins of this walk are first described in his book "James Herriot's Yorkshire", a coffee table book with stunning photographs by Derry Brabbs.

From that informal beginning as a short narration in a book, the walk was expanded and the route modified to include an extra days walking, by Norman Scholes, another devotee of the Yorkshire Dales. Although it is now a well-known long distance path, it has no official status and you will find no "Herriot Way" signposts along the route. However, the route follows established Rights of Way along its whole length, either footpaths or bridleways and these are nearly always signposted clearly.

HOW HARD IS IT?
Of all the questions addressed in this book, this is probably the most difficult one to answer. The main reason being, of course, is that it is so subjective. For an experienced long distance walker, this is merely a training walk, a leg stretcher. For someone who has never walked for four or five days in a row this could be a much more serious undertaking. The difficulty will also be relative to how fit the walker is.

The walk involves a total of approximately 52 miles (84 km) with an overall height gain of around 7,700 feet (2,350 m) and an equal amount of descent of course, as it is a circular walk. The toughest section is likely to be the day that includes the ascent of Great Shunner Fell and although this involves a long steady climb, it is not steep, the path is generally good and is even paved for long sections to protect the peat bogs.

The walk should be well within the limitations of a regular walker or someone with a good level of fitness. The individual day walks themselves are not too arduous, but the fact that they come one after the other in quick succession does mean you need to be adequately prepared.

The only "disclaimer" contained in this book is here; it is the experience of this author that most people are sensible and have a healthy concern for their own good health and well-being. It is with this knowledge that this book contains none of the usual "take care along the road" type warnings that seem to pepper modern publications. The route description is provided on the understanding that anyone walking along a road, for example, will do so with the degree of caution and awareness that any sensible person would employ. End of disclaimer.

HOW MANY DAYS?

The walk is designed around the four villages of Aysgarth, Hawes, Keld and Reeth and as such is generally considered to be a four day walk. This four day itinerary also means the walk is broken down into four approximately equal stages of about 13 miles (21 km) each.

If you are planning this walk yourself then of course you can take as long as you like over it and there are many villages along the route (and slightly off the route) that can be used to break the walk down into smaller stages.

The itinerary planner on page 5 will help you decide where you can stop and how long your stages will be between villages. At the time of publication, all these stops had at least one accommodation provider offering Bed & Breakfast.

Suggested Three-Day Itineraries

Due to the way villages are located along the traditional route it is almost impossible to plan a three-day Herriot Way walk, with equal daily distances, unless you engage the services of a local taxi company.

The best three-day option for the traditional route, using the high path between Keld and Reeth is as follows:

1. Reeth to Askrigg (19m / 31km)
2. Askrigg to Keld (20m / 32km)
3. Keld to Reeth (11m / 18km)

With the first two days being around 20 miles each, this isn't an ideal itinerary, but it will at least allow you to complete the walk in three days without vehicle assistance.

A better three-day option is now available, if you choose to use the new low level route between Keld and Reeth, beside the River Swale. This brings the village of Gunnerside into play and provides this itinerary:

1. Castle Bolton to Hawes (16m / 26km)
2. Hawes to Gunnerside (18m / 29km)
3. Gunnerside to Castle Bolton (17m / 27km)

Five Day Itinerary "Herriot Way Plus"

In bad weather the traditional route between Keld and Reeth can be quite arduous and unlike the route over Great Shunner Fell, which is no better when the rain is hammering down, there is at least a low-level alternative into Reeth.

For many years, Coast to Coast walkers between Keld and Reeth have had the option of taking an easier route alongside the River Swale and it only seems fair that Herriot Way walkers should have the same option. This fourth edition of the guide book sees that omission rectified and a new low-level route option has now been added.

If you have five days to spare you should consider doing both routes between Keld and Reeth; both are splendid in their own rights and with the help of the **Little White Bus** service, and a two-night stay in Keld, this is perfectly possible.

ITINERARY PLANNER

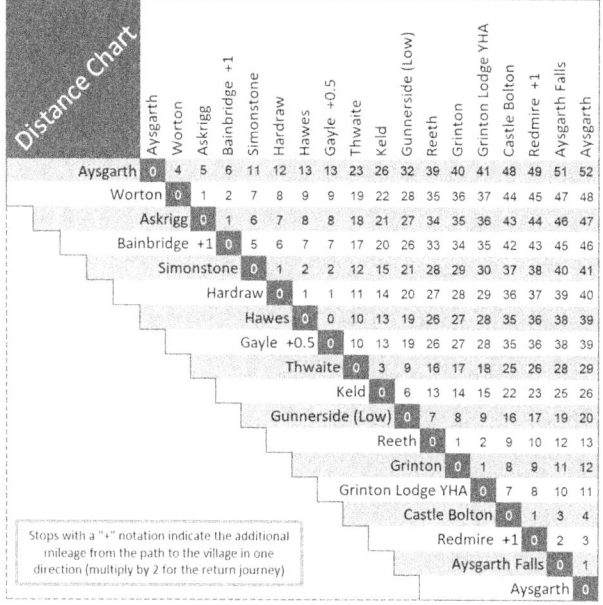

	Aysgarth	Worton	Askrigg	Bainbridge +1	Simonstone	Hardraw	Hawes	Gayle +0.5	Thwaite	Keld	Gunnerside (Low)	Reeth	Grinton	Grinton Lodge YHA	Castle Bolton	Redmire +1	Aysgarth Falls	Aysgarth
Aysgarth	0	4	5	6	11	12	13	13	23	26	32	39	40	41	48	49	51	52
Worton		0	1	2	7	8	9	9	19	22	28	35	36	37	44	45	47	48
Askrigg			0	1	6	7	8	8	18	21	27	34	35	36	43	44	46	47
Bainbridge +1				0	5	6	7	7	17	20	26	33	34	35	42	43	45	46
Simonstone					0	1	2	2	12	15	21	28	29	30	37	38	40	41
Hardraw						0	1	1	11	14	20	27	28	29	36	37	39	40
Hawes							0	0	10	13	19	26	27	28	35	36	38	39
Gayle +0.5								0	10	13	19	26	27	28	35	36	38	39
Thwaite									0	3	9	16	17	18	25	26	28	29
Keld										0	6	13	14	15	22	23	25	26
Gunnerside (Low)											0	7	8	9	16	17	19	20
Reeth												0	1	2	9	10	12	13
Grinton													0	1	8	9	11	12
Grinton Lodge YHA														0	7	8	10	11
Castle Bolton															0	1	3	4
Redmire +1																0	2	3
Aysgarth Falls																	0	1
Aysgarth																		0

Stops with a "+" notation indicate the additional mileage from the path to the village in one direction (multiply by 2 for the return journey)

OVERVIEW

A high-level overview of the route is shown in the map section on page 118, with most of the villages shown along the route. This is not a map you will be able to navigate by, but it may help with the selection of a starting point and the stops you wish to make along the way.

It is worth noting that this scale of OS map is a little out of date and the Youth Hostels in Aysgarth and Keld are no longer running. The hostel in Keld is now in private hands and run as a hotel. Aysgarth has plenty of alternative accommodation, to compensate for the loss of the youth hostel.

Introduction 5

WHERE TO START?

The traditional starting point of the Herriot Way is Aysgarth. This guide describes the walk as starting and ending in Aysgarth as this is the way most walkers will proceed. However, as a circular walk, there is no specific need to start here; you could start at any point along the walk.

Your mode of transport will probably decide your starting point for you. If you're arriving by train, then Hawes may be the most convenient place. Arriving by car will provide the greatest flexibility, but you may then be limited to where you can park the car for four or five days. See the section on "***Getting To and From***" on page 9.

Butt House B&B offer a superb service to Herriot Way walkers. If you stay with them before you set out, or after you finish (or both) you can leave your car in their car park for free, for the duration of your walk.

If you want to start in Aysgarth you can leave your car at the **Falls Coffee Shop**. The car park there is managed by RCP Parking (**www.rcpparking.com**) and you can pay on their website, or using their mobile app. Expect to pay around £25 for a car for four days and slightly more for a campervan.

WHICH DIRECTION?

There is no more reason to walk the path clockwise than there is to walk it anti-clockwise. There is no height gain benefit or prevailing weather considerations as there might be with a linear walk. In fact, the only deciding factor may be the direction this book or other guide books take you.

If you are using a baggage courier service (see the section on "***Support Services***" on page 34) to move your bags from one stop to the next then you will need to check with them if they have a particular direction of travel.

James Herriot originally described a walk taken by him, his son Jimmy and one of his son's friends from Leyburn, through Aysgarth and Askrigg, over Oxnop Common to Keld, up to Gunnerside Gill and then down to the village of Gunnerside then to Low Row, Reeth and Grinton and finally back to Leyburn. Although the route has changed somewhat over the years, it was originally a clockwise walk.

Following that tradition and in order to support the vast majority of walkers; this guide book's walk description and route maps are for the clockwise direction.

WALK SYNOPSIS

The walk, unlike many multi-day walks, is circular; the traditional start and end point being in Aysgarth in the heart of Wensleydale - possibly the most famous of all Yorkshire Dales.

SECTION 1 - AYSGARTH TO HAWES
Distance: Approx 12 miles (19 km)
Height Gain: Approx 900 ft (274 m)

The route heads north out of the village, down to the River Ure, which it follows closely along wide meadows and a disused railway track until turning into Askrigg. This is the village that was used to film the James Herriot TV series. From Askrigg the route travels down the Wensleydale valley, through lush green fields, along narrow, secluded lanes to the village of Hardraw with its famous waterfall and then into Hawes, the largest town on the route and the highest market town in Yorkshire.

SECTION 2 - HAWES TO KELD
Distance: Approx 12½ miles (20 km)
Height Gain: Approx 2800 ft (853 m)

Leaving Hawes, the Way climbs up the side of Great Shunner Fell, the third highest mountain in Yorkshire, following the mostly paved footpath of the Pennine Way, to the summit shelter with wide-ranging views across the surrounding dales and hills and then down into Thwaite. From here the path climbs the slopes of Kisdon and then drops down again into the tiny settlement of Keld.

SECTION 3 - KELD TO REETH (HIGH ROUTE)
Distance: Approx 11 miles (18 km)
Height Gain: Approx 2000 ft (610 m)

Beyond Keld the path says goodbye to rolling green fells and fields and climbs into the bleak and blasted landscape of Gunnerside Moor, changed forever by the lead mining industry that ranged across the moors for decades. The heather however, remains a glorious site despite the industry and now supports the new "industry" of grouse shooting. The Way soon returns to the valley and the wonderful River Swale at Healaugh, before the short walk through fields into Reeth.

SECTION 3 - KELD TO REETH (LOW ROUTE)
Distance: Approx 12 miles (19 km)
Height Gain: Approx 1300 ft (396 m)

From leaving Keld to arriving in Reeth we are never far from the banks of the River Swale and often we are walking hand-in-hand with this iconic river. We drop down through Kisdon Gorge at the head of Swaledale and use paths through the hay meadows to reach Gunnerside. Beyond we cross the Swale and follow riverside paths until we cross again, on Reeth's wonderful footbridge before arriving in the village itself.

SECTION 4 - REETH TO AYSGARTH
Distance: Approx 14 miles (23 km)
Height Gain: Approx 2100 ft (640 m)

Leaving Reeth, the route heads south, climbing up to Grinton Lodge Hostel, right on the edge of the moors. A short hop from the hostel takes the path into the glorious heather and open moorland around Gibbon Hill and then along the rough but easy Apedale Road. After Dent's Houses the path drops steeply down to the village of Castle Bolton and the atmospheric remains of its castle. More fields and back lanes lead to the very impressive falls at Aysgarth and then back to the village itself.

GETTING TO AND FROM

Being a circular walk, the Herriot Way has a significant advantage over most long distance paths, in that there is no requirement to make different arrangements to get to and from the beginning. This is normally one of the biggest logistical problems when planning transport for a long walk.

BY CAR

For many people, this will be the most convenient and probably the quickest way to get to the start of the walk. The larger villages along the route, such as Hawes and Aysgarth, lie directly on the A684 which runs east-west across the Yorkshire Dales and connects the M6 in the west to the A1 in the east. Travellers using the M6 should exit at Junction 37 and those using the M1/A1 should exit at Leeming.

CAR PARKING

If you are travelling by car, you will need somewhere to park it for the duration of your walk. The first port of call should always be the B&B or hotel that you use on the first and/or last day of your walk. Many B&Bs will have somewhere for you to leave your car or know of the best place to leave it within the village such that it causes the least possible inconvenience to residents.

Butt House in **Keld** (**www.butthousekeld.co.uk** or **01748 886374**) will let you leave your car in their car park if you stay with them at the start or end of your walk. Park Lodge farm, also in **Keld**, at the bottom of the village has a large car park, arrange at the shop for your multi-day stay.

The second option will be a public car park, close to your start/finish point. The Yorkshire Dales National Park Authority (YDNPA) owns and manages a number of car parks around the route and there are others run by local councils and independent operators. Charges vary depending on the operator, but YDNPA car parks generally charge around £5 per day for a car. Weekly tickets can also be purchased for YDNPA car parks, but overnight parking varies between locations, so make sure you can leave your car there for the number of days you will be walking.

The YDNPA car parks at **Hawes** and **Aysgarth Falls** allow overnight parking (provided the vehicle is not occupied) and the cost of a weekly ticket is approximately £15. See their website for more details: **www.yorkshiredales.org.uk**

Other car parks can be found in Aysgarth (at the Falls Coffee Shop, see page 6), Askrigg, Hawes, Keld, Muker (a little way off the route, between Thwaite and Keld), Reeth and Castle Bolton. Charges and restrictions will vary for these car parks.

The town with the most flexible and abundant parking is almost certainly **Reeth**, where parking is allowed on and around the large village green, with a voluntary donation of £2 requested for the day.

The final option and one that should be considered with great care, is street parking in the town or village that you have selected as your start/finish point. Please think about the impact your car will have on local residents and their ability to park in their own village. Consider also that some places that may look like convenient parking places will be used by farm vehicles and buses for turning around or accessing gates. Tractors towing trailers for example need lots of room to swing in and out of fields and a parked car could prevent the farmer from conducted business. Narrow lanes often have passing places that look like convenient parking spots but are designed to let farm vehicles and cars pass safely in opposite directions.

BY TRAIN
None of the towns or villages along the route has a train station. The nearest station is Garsdale, which is about 7 miles from Hawes on the Herriot Way. Garsdale station is on the main Leeds to Carlisle line and trains run every two hours or so from Leeds, whilst trains from Carlisle to Garsdale run approximately every three hours. More details can be found at the very informative **www.thetrainline.com** website.

From Garsdale station you can catch the Little White Bus service into Hawes, see next page for details.

You could also use footpaths to walk to Hawes, completely avoiding any busy roads. Use the Pennine Bridleway from the station to the Moorcock Inn, then the path past Yore House to Thwaite Bridge. Cross the road and pass Mossdale Head and Hollin Bank to reach the road at New Bridge. Turn right beside the road towards Appersett and then down the lane to Appersett Viaduct where a footpath across the fields leads to the farm at Ashes and the outskirts of Hawes.

BY COACH

National Express coaches do not venture anywhere close to the Herriot Way and like the mainline train services, they would need to be used in conjunction with other local services to reach a point on the route. The closest coach station would be Kendal, but the most useful destinations would probably be Leeds or Carlisle.

BY BUS

A local bus service runs from Garsdale station to Hawes; operated by the Little White Bus it makes about four runs a day Monday to Saturday, with a reduced service on a Sunday. The runs are mostly scheduled to coincide with the train arrivals and departures at Garsdale and the bus will generally wait a reasonable time for delayed trains. More details of this service can be found on the Dales Bus website, which is here: **www.dalesbus.org**

There are a number of bus services that could be used to get close to the Herriot Way and indeed some will stop at points along the route, primarily in Wensleydale (Hawes and Aysgarth) and Swaledale (Reeth). These change too often to include route details in this book. The Dales Bus website has the best source of local bus service information and can be found here: **www.dalesbus.org**

BY TAXI

You may wish to, or possibly need to, use a taxi for the final leg of the journey to the starting point of the Herriot Way. Public transport may be able to get you most of the way and there are some bus services that will get you all the way, but the closer you get to your destination, the less convenient and regular schedules become.

Always ensure you ride with a licensed taxi driver. The local regulatory authority will require the taxi to display a license plate on the rear of the vehicle and for the driver to display his badge in the cab. All licensed taxis will also have a meter, to ensure a fair and consistent charge for the journey.

Private Hire Vehicles, distinct from taxis, cannot carry passengers unless booked in advance, so you will not be able to pick one up outside the station for example. PHVs may not have a meter and you should always agree the fare before the journey begins. Feel free to haggle with the operator when you make the booking, but double-check this price with the driver when you meet them.

It's worth remembering that you are unlikely to be able to pay for a taxi or PHV with anything other than cash, unless you are paying for a PHV in advance.

WHEN TO WALK

UK PUBLIC HOLIDAYS
The UK has eight public holidays, also called Bank Holidays. These days fall either on a Monday or a Friday and don't generally occur on a specific date (except Christmas); rather the dates are set by the government two or three years in advance.

Some of the public holidays occur during prime walking months; Easter, early spring and late summer and as a result the availability of accommodation may be restricted on these weekends. Some businesses, banks in particular, will also be closed on these days. Restricted public transport schedules will also be in place. For a full list of dates for this year and the next two years refer to the UK Government website here: **www.gov.uk**

WEATHER
Unfortunately, the UK is not blessed with the sort of climate that allows a walker to say, "I will walk in such-and-such a month to ensure good weather". We are as likely to see glorious sunny days in December as we are in July and similarly snow has been recorded in almost every month of the year in the Yorkshire Dales.

However, as a general rule, the weather is likely to be warmer between May and September than at any other time of the year. Rain, wind, low cloud, mist and fog are year-round occurrences and anyone who has walked in the UK before will be used to this.

A sound philosophy is to "hope for the best and prepare for the worst". This means carrying appropriate cold weather gear such as hats and gloves, especially for the section over Great Shunner Fell, which at 2,349 feet (716m) is the third highest point in any of the Yorkshire Ridings.

The following climate charts provide a view of the average recorded conditions for the Yorkshire area over the past few years.

DAYLIGHT AND SUNSHINE AVERAGES

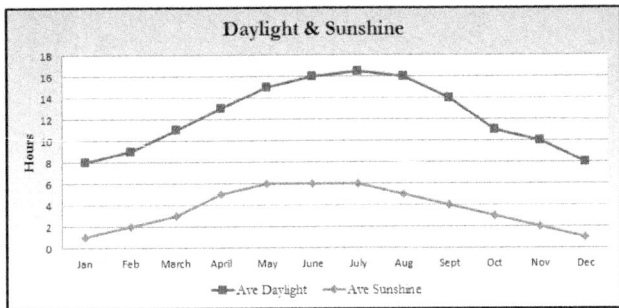

The relatively low mileages that are involved each day mean that most walkers will be able to complete the route during daylight hours even in the darkest winter months.

TEMPERATURE AVERAGES

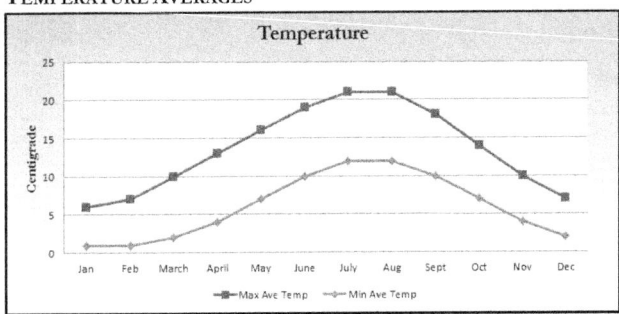

The temperature chart does not take account of any windchill that may be experienced, especially on the higher, more exposed parts of the route. In cold and wet conditions, windchill can significantly reduce the experienced temperature and even in summer, can contribute to hypothermia.

RAINFALL AVERAGES

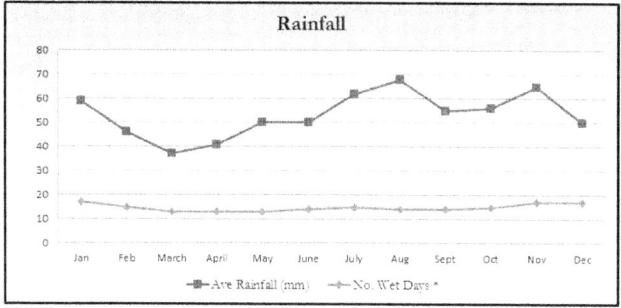

* The number of wet days indicates the number of days that experienced more than ¼ mm of rain.

GROUSE SHOOTING

Large sections of the walk cross the open heather moorlands that now support one of the staple "industries" of the Dales; Grouse Shooting. As you walk along the Herriot Way, you will see many grouse butts; low stone or wooden structures, normally semi-circular that provide cover for the individual shooters. Many of their walls are topped with heather or turf to help them blend into the surroundings, whether this is to hide their presence from the unsuspecting grouse, or to soften their impact on the environment is unclear.

Some of the roads and tracks you walk along are constructed to support the four-wheel drive vehicles that transport the shooters to the fells. You will even come across the occasional shooting hut; a building that provides shelter for shooters during bad weather or for lunch breaks.

All this infrastructure supports a four-month grouse shooting season; starting on the "Glorious 12th" of August each year, as parties of shooters, guides, beaters and other support staff head to the moors to shoot the grouse.

If you are walking between 12th August and 10th December, there is a small chance your walk may be delayed or diverted to avoid shooting parties. If you hear shooting close by, keep an eye open for men with red flags, who are there to warn you if you are about to stray too close to a shoot. Do not be turned back, be aware of your rights and make sure you are on the PRoW. The Natural England website (now part of the UK Government website) has more information on PRoW, which can be found here: **www.gov.uk**

FLORA IN THE DALES

There are two particularly special times to walk in the Dales; late May/early June and late August/early September. In late spring and early summer, the fields in the valleys will be full of flowering plants and grasses; a veritable explosion of colour all around you with a narrow green path between. These meadows supply the winter feed for the livestock.

In late summer the heather flowers on the moors and the normally brown landscape turns purple for a few short weeks. This is one of the most magical times to walk the high paths in the Dales.

A word about website links (URLs)

Full addresses for websites mentioned in this book can be found on the book's website: **www.herriotway.com**

GENERAL WALKING ADVICE

A BEGINNERS' GUIDE
The Herriot Way will be the first multi-day walk for many people so this section will cover some advice that will seem quite obvious to experienced long distance walkers, but may still prove useful to beginners.

Footwear: You'll notice the avoidance of the word boot! Boots are not essential for this walk and a comfortable pair of approach shoes, trail shoes or fell running shoes will be adequate. Many people prefer to walk in boots at all times and this is the crux of this piece of advice; walk in what you are most comfortable in. Never use a multi-day walk to try untested shoes or boots. For other kit related advice, see the section on "***Kit***" on page 23.

Maps: There are some sections of this walk where finding the right path or walking in the right direction could be tricky if the mist rolls in or the cloud layer drops. If this happens it's important that you can find your way down off the fells comfortably. Always walk with an Ordnance Survey (or similar) map that covers a wide area around the walk route. The maps in this book will lead you along the path, but will not help if you go astray and find yourself walking in uncharted territory. Mark the map with possible "escape" routes; quick exits off the high hills down to a road or village. Don't be afraid to use these routes; it's better to be at the bottom of the hill wishing you were on the top, than on the top wishing you were at the bottom. See the section on "***Navigation***" on page 38.

Compass and GPS: A map will only help so much without a compass or GPS device. Carry one or the other and know how to use it. If you're using a compass, use it regularly; take bearings when you can, especially in mist. If using a GPS check the battery level every morning and make sure you can get a satellite lock before leaving. See the section on "***Navigation***" on page 38.

Weather: The weather on the hills can change quickly, so always try and get a local weather forecast before you leave.

Good B&Bs will be able to provide this or the local Tourist Information Office will also have one posted in clear view. If the weather is likely to be foul and you are not confident in route finding in bad conditions, then consider an alternative low-level route.

Walking Time: Allow plenty of time to get to your destination. An average walking pace is about three miles per hour, but when you factor in lunch and other rest stops, taking photographs, hill ascents, admiring the scenery and all the other little interruptions you will probably not average much more than two miles per hour and often less.

BEING SAFE
Let your B&B owner know where you are heading next and the name of the place you will be staying at. Make sure the owner of the B&B you are heading to knows roughly what sort of time to expect you. If you don't arrive you can expect a responsible landlady to call Mountain Rescue.

WHAT TO DO IN AN EMERGENCY
If you know you're going to be delayed, but it isn't an emergency, for example you've descended into the wrong valley; make sure you inform your accommodation for that evening, or anyone else who may be expecting you. This will hopefully ensure that Mountain (or Fell) Rescue isn't called out unnecessarily.

In the event of an injury to a member of your party try and give the casualty appropriate basic first aid; make sure their breathing is not obstructed, try and staunch any blood flow with items from your first aid kit and keep them warm and dry if at all possible. See the section on "***Kit***" on page 23.

Send for help. If you have a mobile phone signal dial 999 and ask for the Police. Give as many details of your location as you can to the operator, including an OS Grid Reference if possible. If you have no phone signal make your way to a telephone box or the nearest habitation. If you call the Police from a box, stay there; you may need to guide rescuers to the location of the casualty. In most cases the Police will call out the nearest Mountain (or Fell) Rescue Team.

MOUNTAIN RESCUE
The Yorkshire Dales National Park is covered by several mountain rescue teams. For information on their work, fundraising and other activities, visit their websites using the links below:

- Upper Wharfedale Fell Rescue Association (UWFRA)
  www.uwfra.org.uk
- Cave Rescue Organisation (CRO)
  www.cro.org.uk
- Swaledale Mountain Rescue Team
  www.swaledalemrt.org.uk
- Kirkby Stephen Mountain Rescue Team
  www.kirkbystephenmrt.org.uk

DEHYDRATION
The symptoms of dehydration include headaches, muscle cramps, decreased blood pressure and dizziness or fainting when standing up. If left untreated dehydration can result in delirium, poor decision making and possibly unconsciousness.

Dehydration symptoms generally become noticeable after 2% of one's normal water volume has been lost. Initially, one experiences thirst and discomfort, possibly along with loss of appetite. One may also notice decreased urine volume, abnormally dark urine or unexplained tiredness. The simple way to avoid dehydration is to drink regularly and don't wait to feel thirsty, especially in warm weather.

DRINKING FROM STREAMS
As the route is essentially a low-level route and almost completely grazed by sheep or cattle, the water sources along the route should not be trusted. Unless you can find a spring at its source, all water collected on the route should be treated before drinking. The close proximity of villages and towns along the route should enable campers to collect fresh water regularly from these sources.

General Walking Advice

WALKING WITH A DOG

The Herriot Way, along its whole length, uses Public Rights of Way (PRoW), whether they are footpaths or bridleways. This means that, providing you follow the route described in this book, there are no restrictions to walking with a dog.

Where the PRoW crosses Open Access land (see below) and that land is used for grazing sheep or raising grouse then you may be requested to keep your dog under close control and probably on a lead, especially during the period from 1st March to 31st July when animals and birds are raising young.

Although there are no restrictions to walking with your dog, you may find logistical problems along sections of the walk, especially through Wensleydale, as many of the stiles are very narrow. Pinch stiles are narrow gaps in the dry stone walls designed to prevent stock moving between fields, without using a gate. As such, large dogs may struggle to fit and you may have to lift them over the wall.

As well as the pinch stiles, there are many gated step stiles through the walls. These are wider but have two or three protruding stones that act as steps on each side, with a spring-loaded gate at the top to protect the gap. These can be awkward to use with a dog.

Pinch stile (left) and gated wall stile (right)

COWS

Sections of this walk, particularly between Hawes and Aysgarth, will pass through fields containing livestock; some of these may hold cows. In the vast majority of cases they will pay no attention to walkers other than to lift their heads to monitor your progress. Cows, simply due to their size alone, should always be treated with caution however, give them room and avoid coming up from behind and startling them.

Cows with calves should be treated with special care and always try to avoid walking between a cow and her calf, they may see this as a threat. Cows have an instinctive distrust of dogs and may react unpredictably to a dog in their field. Keep your dog under close control, but if cows approach you and become aggressive towards your dog; allow the dog to run free, it will almost certainly be able to outrun an attacking cow and will also divert their interest away from you.

Young cows will often dash across a field to investigate you, but they usually stop a little way off. Resist the urge to run away from an approaching cow or cows. If they approach too close, turn and face them and if necessary wave your hands and shout at them. Make your way to the nearest exit, which may be the way you entered the field and make alternative arrangements to rejoin the path.

You may also encounter bulls in fields with a public footpath, but in general these are no more problematic than cows. A bull with cows is typically quite docile and should present no problem at all. Take more care with a lone bull, however, and give them as wide a berth as possible.

The Ramblers, a UK charity that supports walkers, has specific advice on walking through fields with cows and other animals and this can be found here: **www.ramblers.org.uk**

OPEN ACCESS

As has already been mentioned, the Herriot Way does not rely on the rights granted to walkers under the Countryside and Rights of Way Act 2000, which identified large areas of previously private land and made it "Open Access Land".

However, it does use Rights of Way that cross Open Access Land, so it's worth being aware of what it is.

This symbol denotes the beginning of Access land and you will see it posted on gates and stiles. A similar sign with a red line through it marks the end of Access land.

Access land, as described in the 2000 Act, includes open country; i.e. mountains, moorland, heath and down, common land and other land dedicated as part of the Act. There are some exceptions to these broad definitions and not all Access land is open at all times. The Natural England website has more information on Open Access, which can be found here: **www.gov.uk**

Walking on Access land can be challenging and dangerous, you will often be a long way from recognised paths or obvious landmarks. Stiles and gates may also be few and far between. As a large percentage of the access land is open moorland, good navigation skills are required.

The latest editions of 1:25k Ordnance Survey maps show open access land with a pale yellow shading.

TICKS AND TICK-BORNE DISEASES
The Herriot Way route doesn't fall into one of the UK hotspots for ticks, but there's always the chance that you could pick up one of these little parasites whilst walking. There are a number of different tick-borne diseases, but the most common is Lyme Disease (Borreliosis).

It is important to know the best way to remove a tick and therefore the best way to avoid Lyme Disease once you have a tick attached. A specialist tick removal tool is the best implement to use and these can be purchased cheaply from outdoor shops. They weigh next to nothing and are easy to carry "just in case".

More information on how to avoid ticks, how to remove them and the diseases they carry can be found at the British Mountaineering Council website; which is here: **www.thebmc.co.uk**

KIT

As this may be the first multi-day walk for some people, the following list includes some guidance on why the items mentioned may be useful. This should not be considered a definitive list; merely a guide to what a walker may want to consider when walking in the hills.

This list is appropriate for someone who is using a baggage courier to move the bulk of their kit; these are the sort of items you may want to carry on a day-to-day basis.

Rucksack: If you are using a baggage courier (see section on "***Support Services***" on page 34) you can get away with a standard day pack, this will probably need to be about 25 litres in capacity. Make sure any pack you buy sits comfortably with items in it; worth testing in the shop.

Footwear: You'll notice the avoidance of the word boot! Boots are not essential for this walk, although many people are happy to walk in boots at all times and you should wear what you're most comfortable in. The paths are generally good on the Herriot Way and a comfortable pair of approach shoes, trail shoes or fell running shoes will be adequate.

Waterproof Jacket: One of the first items that should go into any pack; the weather in the UK demands that suitable waterproof clothing be carried at all times. When buying a waterproof jacket, consider how packable it is; how much room will it take up in your pack and how much does it weigh?

Waterproof Overtrousers: Almost as important as a waterproof jacket; these will keep your lower body dry and warm. Not as essential in the summer, but an important item for the rest of the year.

Warm Hat & Gloves: Irrespective of what time of the year you are walking, always take some cold weather gear, especially if your route involves a big hill like Great Shunner Fell. The weather on the tops can change quickly. Consider a dry bag for storing the gear, this keeps it dry in the event of rain.

Lunch & Water: If you are walking all day you will need to refuel at some point. If you're venturing high and away from habitation, plan on carrying enough food for an emergency night on the hills. An average day walk of six hours or so is also going to require about 2 litres of water, but take more if the weather is hot and sunny; dehydration is a very real problem.

Survival Shelter: This is really a "nice to have" rather than an essential item. A survival shelter is essentially a large waterproof bag big enough for a couple of people to sit inside knee to knee across from each other. It helps establish a safe temperature environment in really bad conditions, but it's also great for when it's raining at lunch time.

Whistle: A mountain whistle is essential for anyone walking on the hills. It can be used to attract the attention of a rescue team coming to help you, but can also be used to alert other walkers that someone needs assistance. The emergency signal is six blasts on the whistle; repeated every minute. The response is three short blasts. Continue to signal even if you hear the response, it will help guide rescuers onto your location.

Head torch: Always useful to have; just in case you ever get delayed and end up walking off the hills after dark. With the advent of LED technology, torches are now very small and very light.

First aid kit: Most supermarket-bought first aid kits will be fine for this purpose. You really need plasters, one or two small bandages, anti-septic wipes and cream and perhaps a sling and some tape. You may wish to add some blister plasters and some pain killers, but it's pointless carrying anything you don't know how to use.

Mobile phone: Although you may not get a signal in the hills, this may still be useful. SMS text messages require significantly less signal than a call, so even when a call is impossible, a text message may still get through. See page 36 for information on mobile emergency roaming.

Sunglasses: Glare causes headaches and can seriously ruin your day, it can be even worse in winter with snow on the ground.

Sunhat & Sun Cream: Think positive!

Waterproof Map Case: This helps keep your map dry and also provides a convenient method for carrying what can be an awkward item, especially if you're using the full OS map.

Compass and/or GPS: It's all very well having the map, but unless you know where you are it's not going to help you very much. The same advice applies to both the compass and the GPS; make sure you know how to use it, before you need to use it.

Kendal Mint Cake: Very few people carry this because they like it, but its weight to calorific value ratio is high and it has a long shelf (or pack) life, so you can leave it in the bottom of your rucksack until the day you actually need it.

HOSTELS AND B&BS

HOSTELS
There are only two Youth Hostels Association premises serving the Herriot Way now. The hostels in Aysgarth and Keld have both been sold off in previous years, leaving Grinton Lodge (just outside Grinton) and Hawes.

You no longer have to be a member of the YHA to use their hostels, but non-members pay a temporary membership fee for each night they use a hostel, this is normally about £3.

GRINTON
Address: Grinton Lodge YH, Grinton, DL11 6HS
Tel: 0845 371 9636
Email: grinton@yha.org.uk
Web site: **www.yha.org.uk**
OS Grid Ref: SE 047 975
Note: Grinton Lodge is located ½ a mile south of Grinton on the Leyburn road

HAWES
Address: Lancaster Terrace, Hawes, DL8 3LQ
Tel: 0845 371 9120
Email: hawes@yha.org.uk
Web site: **www.yha.org.uk**
OS Grid Ref: SD 868 898

BED AND BREAKFAST (B&B)
The route is well supported by Bed and Breakfast accommodation, most of it well used to catering to walkers. The list below gives a sample of those available and should not be considered exhaustive by any means. Similarly, inclusion in the list does not signify a recommendation by the author.

AYSGARTH
Cornlee Guest House
Proprietor: Jayson Banham
Address: Cornlee, Aysgarth, DL8 3AE
Tel: 01969 663779
Email: stay@cornlee.co.uk

Web site: **www.cornlee.co.uk**
OS Grid Ref: SE 004 884

Yoredale House
Proprietor: Steve and Sandra Hamilton
Address: Aysgarth, DL8 3AE
Tel: 01969 663423
Email: info@yoredalehouse.com
Web site: **www.yoredalehouse.com**
OS Grid Ref: SE 003 884

Wensleydale Farmhouse B&B
Proprietor: Sheila and Bruce Toper
Address: Aysgarth, DL8 3SR
Tel: 01969 663534
Email: stay@wensleydale-farmhouse.co.uk
Web site: **www.wensleydale-farmhouse.co.uk**
OS Grid Ref: SE 011 883
Note: Located 0.6 miles outside Aysgarth village, by the road to Aysgarth Falls.

HAWES
Spring Bank House B&B
Proprietor: Eric and Debra Kenyon
Address: Burtersett Road, Hawes, DL8 3NT
Tel: 01969 667376
Email: debraeric@aol.com
Web site: **www.springbankhousehawes.co.uk**
OS Grid Ref: SD 875 897

Crosby House B&B
Proprietor: Mike and Claudia
Address: Burtersett Road, Hawes, DL8 3NP
Tel: 01969 667322
Email: book@crosbyhousehawes.co.uk
Web site: **www.crosbyhousehawes.co.uk**
OS Grid Ref: SD 876 897

White Hart Country Inn
Proprietor: Matthew Kirkbride
Address: Main Street, Hawes, DL8 3QL
Tel: 01969 667214

Email: matt@whitehartcountryinn.co.uk
Web site: **www.whitehartcountryinn.co.uk**
OS Grid Ref: SD 873 898

KELD
Keld Lodge
Proprietor: Nick & Karen Glanvill
Address: Keld Lodge, Keld, DL11 6LL
Tel: 01748 886259
Email: info@keldlodge.com
Web site: **www.keldlodge.com**
OS Grid Ref: NY 891 009

Butt House B&B
Proprietor: Jacqui & Chris Giles
Address: Butt House, Keld, DL11 6LL
Tel: 01748 886374
Email: info@butthousekeld.co.uk
Web site: **www.butthousekeld.co.uk**
OS Grid Ref: NY 893 009

OUTSIDE KELD
Greenlands B&B
Proprietor: Mark and Jude Waterton
Address: Angram Lane, Keld, DL11 6DY
Tel: 01748 886532 or 07917 391236
Email: greenlandskeld@btinternet.com
Web site: **www.greenlandskeld.co.uk**
OS Grid Ref: NY 888 000

REETH
Cambridge House B&B
Proprietor: Robert & Sheila Mitchell
Address: Arkengarthdale Road, Reeth, DL11 6QX
Tel: 01748 884633
Email: info@cambridgehousereeth.co.uk
Web site: **www.cambridgehousereeth.co.uk**
OS Grid Ref: SE 036 998

Springfield House B&B
Proprietor: Denise Guy
Address: Quaker Close, Reeth, DL11 6UY

Tel:	01748 884634
Email:	denisem.guy@btinternet.com
Web site:	**www.springfield-house.co.uk**
OS Grid Ref:	SE 039 993

Buck Hotel
Address:	Silver Street, Reeth, DL11 6SW
Tel:	01748 884210
Email:	buckhotel@btinternet.com
Web site:	**www.buckhotel.co.uk**
OS Grid Ref:	SE 038 993

There is also plenty of additional accommodation just off the main route, within easy walking distance of the path and these may be less busy because of that. If you try and book a B&B and are told it's full; the proprietor will almost certainly be happy to recommend alternative establishments nearby, don't be afraid to ask the question.

CAMPING

CAMP SITES

There are quite a few camp sites scattered along the Herriot Way route and several more just off the usual route. It is certainly possible to camp the whole route using organised camp sites.

The following should not be considered a definitive list by any means; camp sites come and go, but the list was accurate at the time of publishing. Where possible, details of Email addresses and Web site addresses have been included, but some camp sites can only be contacted by telephone.

By far and away the best resource for finding information about the nearest camp sites, the facilities they have and reviews from campers is the UK Campsite website. You can search by name, location or even view camp sites on an interactive map. **www.ukcampsite.co.uk**

AYSGARTH
Aysgarth Falls Hotel
Tel: 01969 663775
Open: April to end October
Email: info@aysgarthfallshotel.com
Website: **www.aysgarthfallshotel.com**
OS Grid Ref: SE 015 881
Note: Tents only. Located on the corner of the A684 and Church Bank (the road to the falls)

Colman's of Aysgarth
Tel: 01969 662666
Email: info@aysgarthcamping.co.uk
Website: **www.aysgarthcamping.co.uk**
OS Grid Ref: SE 005 883

HAWES
Bainbridge Ings Country Park
Tel: 01969 667354
Open: April to October
Email: info@bainbridge-ings-countrypark.co.uk

Web site: **bainbridge-ings-countrypark.co.uk**
OS Grid Ref: SD 880 894

Hardraw
The Green Dragon Inn Campsite
Tel: 01969 667392
Open: All year
Email: thegreendragoninnhardraw@gmail.com
Web site: **www.thegreendragoninnhardraw.com**
OS Grid Ref: SD 867 912
Note: Tents only

Old Hall Cottage Campsite
Telephone: 01969 667691
Open: Easter to end October
Email: info@oldhallcottagecampsite.co.uk
Web site: **oldhallcottagecampsite.co.uk**
OS Grid Ref: SD 866 911
Note: Tents, Caravans, Motorhomes

Shaw Ghyll Farm (Simonstone)
Tel: 01969 667359
Open: April to October
Email: info@shawghyll.co.uk
Web site: **www.shawghyll.co.uk**
OS Grid Ref: SD 867 919
Note: Tents, Caravans, Motorhomes. Located 0.7 miles north of Hardraw in Simonstone

Muker
Usha Gap Caravans & Camping
Tel: 01748 886110
Open: All year
Email: info@ushagap.co.uk
Web site: **www.ushagap.co.uk**
OS Grid Ref: SD 902 979
Note: Tents, Caravans, Motorhomes. This is located 0.7 miles east of Thwaite, off the Herriot Way path.

Keld
Park Lodge
Tel: 01748 886274

Email:	rukins@btinternet.com
Web site:	**www.rukins-keld.co.uk**
OS Grid Ref:	NY 893 012

Swaledale Yurts
Tel:	01748 886549
Open:	All year
E-mail:	info@swaledaleyurts.com
Web site:	**www.swaledaleyurts.com**
OS Grid Ref:	NY 887 014
Note:	Tents, Caravans, Motorhomes. This is located ½ a mile west of Keld on the B6270

REETH
Orchard Caravan & Camping
Tel:	01748 884475 or 07397 302277
Open:	April to October
Email:	office@orchardcaravanpark.com
Web site:	**www.orchardcaravanpark.com**
OS Grid Ref:	SE 039 988
Note:	Tents, Caravans, Motorhomes

WILD CAMPING

In England, wild camping is still essentially illegal, without seeking the permission of the landowner first. However, farmers tend to accept that wild camping happens on their land. The general rule of thumb should be to camp above the last intake wall, pitch late and depart early and leave no trace of your stay. In most cases, if you abide by these guidelines the farmer will never know you were there.

Large sections of the Herriot Way do not lend themselves easily to wild camping following these guidelines. The section between Aysgarth and Hawes is primarily low level walking through fields and pastures; most of which will be occupied by sheep, cattle or other livestock. Some farms may let you camp, but you should certainly seek approval along this section.

The sections of the walk over high ground will provide much better opportunities to pitch. Between Hawes and Keld (apart from the fields around Thwaite) the majority of the path lies beyond the last intake wall and although the ground is mostly heather covered, you will find camping places.

Similarly from Keld (after Crackpot Hall) to Surrender Bridge (and slightly beyond) there is plenty of wide open space to camp. Many of the old mining buildings along this section will also provide additional shelter for the tent.

From Surrender Bridge to Grinton the route is again fairly low level and not suitable for a wild camp unless you manage to secure permission from a farmer.

From Grinton the path again follows a high level route and camping opportunities are numerous, all the way to Castle Bolton. From here to Aysgarth we are again walking through fields and pastures.

WATER

As the route is essentially a low-level route and almost completely grazed by sheep and cattle, the water sources along the route should not be trusted. Even the high level sections over Great Shunner Fell, Gunnerside Moor and Gibbon Hill are not really high enough to guarantee that fast running streams are not contaminated. There is also the added deterrent of the water colour from these sources - most rivers will be stained brown by the peat.

Unless you can find a spring at its source, all water collected on the route should be treated before drinking. The close proximity of villages and towns along the route should enable campers to collect fresh water regularly.

SUPPORT SERVICES

BAGGAGE TRANSFER

Over the past few years a small industry has blossomed along the National Trails and Long Distance Paths in the UK; the baggage transfer business. Carrying everything you require for a multi-day walk can be an arduous task and can often be a barrier to some people walking a long distance path. There is now an answer; the baggage couriers.

The baggage courier will collect your bag from the B&B in the morning and move it along the trail to your next stop. Your overnight bag is hand delivered from one door to the other and all you need to carry each day is your normal day-walk pack with its usual essential items.

Some baggage couriers have gone an extra step and now offer package holiday bookings. They will book your accommodation for you and carry your luggage between stops. If you don't have the time or the inclination to contact B&Bs to create your own holiday, there are companies out there that will do it all for you. You just need to decide how many days you want to spend walking the route.

FULL HOLIDAY PACKAGE

These companies will book your accommodation and carry your luggage.

Brigantes Walking Holidays

Tel: 01756 770402
E-mail: info@bagmovers.com
Web site: **www.brigantesenglishwalks.com**
Note: Baggage Transfer is available separately from Accommodation Booking. Brigantes will support you in both directions and you can start at any point along the route.

Mickledore Travel

Tel: 017687 72335
E-mail: info@mickledore.co.uk
Web site: **www.mickledore.co.uk**
Note: Baggage Transfer is only available as part of the Full Holiday Package

Contours Holidays
Tel: 01629 821900
E-mail: info@contours.co.uk
Web site: **www.contours.co.uk**
Note: Baggage Transfer is only available as part of the Full Holiday Package

BAGGAGE TRANSFER ONLY
Brigantes Walking Holidays
Tel: 01756 770402
E-mail: info@bagmovers.com
Web site: **www.brigantesenglishwalks.com**

MONEY
The availability of cash along the route is not great. The major high street banks have long since abandoned the smaller towns and villages of rural communities and the Yorkshire Dales were not exempt from this process. The last remaining bank, Barclays in Hawes, finally closed its doors in July 2019.

CASH BACK
The only way to get cash is to buy something with a Debit Card, with which some establishments may provide "cash back" on top of your purchase. There is normally a minimum spend associated with this service and is typically provided by larger supermarkets.

TOILETS
The Yorkshire Dales National Park Authority manages a number of public toilets across the National Park, as do local councils and other independent providers. A list of the toilets, both official and unofficial, to be found along the route is included here.

- Askrigg (in the Temperance Hall)
- Aysgarth Falls (in the National Park Centre)
- Castle Bolton (in the castle's car park)
- Dent's Houses (in the larger of the two shooting huts south of the bridge)
- Grinton (on the B6270, behind the Bridge Inn)

- Hardraw (in the Green Dragon, if visiting the falls)
- Hawes (main street, next to the small car park)
- Keld (on the road into the village from the B6270)
- Reeth (north end (top) of the village green)

Remember that all public houses will have toilets, but also be aware that unless you are buying a drink or a meal in the pub, it is good etiquette to ask the landlord if you can use their facilities.

MOBILE PHONES AND TELEPHONE BOXES

Most people carry a mobile phone when walking, even if they wouldn't carry one in normal life. They can be critical when trying to request assistance on the fells, or indeed just for keeping in touch with loved ones back home.

The EE network has the best overall coverage for the Herriot Way, with O2 coming a close second. You can pick up an EE SIM card for an unlocked mobile phone from any EE shop. They are normally free if you buy a small amount of credit at the same time. You can also apply online for a SIM using their website.

MOBILE EMERGENCY ROAMING

In October 2009, Ofcom, the UK telephone regulator, finally agreed plans for an emergency mobile roaming service in the UK. This allows a mobile phone to use any available network for emergency calls in the event of no signal being available from the phone's primary network provider. Simply dial 999 or 112 to access the service. You don't need credit on the phone to make an emergency call.

Mobile emergency roaming has its limitations though. You will not be able to receive a call using the service unless you can get a signal from the provider to which your phone is registered, so the emergency services may not be able to call you back for example. The mobile phone also needs to have a registered and activated SIM card in it to use the service.

You can now access 999 services via SMS text message, provided you have registered for the Emergency SMS service.

Registration is free, but must be completed before you use the service. See more details here: **www.emergencysms.org.uk**

TELEPHONE BOXES

Many of the towns and villages along the route will include a telephone box among the local amenities, indeed with the closure of so many rural shops and pubs, this is sometimes the only amenity in a village.

In a bid to reduce the amount of maintenance they need and to prevent them being a target for vandals and thieves, some telephone boxes no longer take coins. Instead you will need a credit or debit card to make a call.

Details of how to make calls using a debit or credit card will be included on the notice board within the telephone box.

Telephone box locations along the route:

Location	Distance	Location	Distance
Aysgarth	On route	**Appersett**	200 yds
Askrigg	On route	**Thwaite**	On route
Worton	150 yds	**Keld**	On route
Simonstone	150 yds	**Healaugh**	On route
Sedbusk	On route	**Reeth**	On route
Hardraw	On route	**Grinton**	On route
Hawes	On route	**Castle Bolton**	On route
Gayle	0.5 m		

NAVIGATION

MAPS
The Herriot Way is probably one of the only multi-day walks that you can do with the aid of a single Ordnance Survey Explorer map. The Explorer series of maps are the most detailed maps produced by the OS and have a scale of 10cm to 2.5km, or 1:25,000 scale. Maps with the OL (Outdoor Leisure) prefix, cover the UK National Parks and Areas of Outstanding Natural Beauty (AONBs).

The Herriot Way is completely covered by OS Explorer OL30. This can be obtained from most high street outdoor shops or online from bookshops such as Amazon. Specialist map retailers may be able to provide it cheaper, so shop around.

The maps in this guide will enable you to walk the route, but they do assume that you are sticking to the route described and you don't wander off the route by accident or design. It would be advisable to carry the OS map in the event that you stray from the described route, or you need to visit places or walk paths outside the scope of this guide.

DIGITAL MAPPING
There are a number of software packages available on the market today that provide Ordnance Survey maps for a PC or mobile phone. The two most well-known are Memory Map (**www.memory-map.co.uk**) for the PC and ViewRanger (**www.viewranger.com**) for mobile devices. Maps are supplied not in traditional paper format, but electronically on USB media or digital download. The maps are then loaded into a dedicated app, normally supplied with the maps, where you can view them, print them and work with them.

The Herriot Way walk appears on no maps, not even the OS Explorer OL30. The walk is not officially recognised in any way and therefore is not included on maps in the same way that the Pennine Way is for instance. With digital mapping you can print a set of maps very easily, that include a highlighted route such as the Herriot Way. The route is available for download from the website that supports this book (**www.herriotway.com**) and this can be loaded into the digital mapping software of your choice and then printed or loaded into a GPS (see below).

GPS
GPS stands for Global Positioning System and has come to mean a handheld device that receives signals transmitted from orbiting satellites and converts them into a grid reference for your current position. You can upload multiple grid references (or waypoints) to the handheld device and join them together to create a route. When you are out on the hills, the handheld GPS unit will tell you how far and in which direction you need to walk to reach your next waypoint.

The Herriot Way is not the sort of walk where a GPS is an essential item of equipment. However, many people use GPS devices as a matter of course when walking and they are certainly an aid to navigation.

The website for this guide book can be found at **www.herriotway.com** and includes GPS waypoints for the whole of the Herriot Way, which can be downloaded free.

WATERFALLS OF THE HERRIOT WAY

HARDRAW FORCE

Perhaps the most well-known of all the high falls in Yorkshire, Hardraw Force can also be the most spectacular. The drop of around 98 feet is reputed to be the highest, above ground, single drop waterfall in England. You have to go underground, to Gaping Gill near Ingleborough to see water fall, unbroken, from a greater height.

For many years the waterfall has been in the grounds of the Green Dragon Inn and in order to view the falls you need to pay a small entrance fee. The fee paid, you walk along a well maintained path, past the newly built Visitors Centre and along Hardraw Beck to the foot of the falls.

As you do so you follow in the footsteps of writers and artists such as William Wordsworth and John Turner and modern day counterparts including Mark Hamill and Kevin Costner. Turner painted the falls in around 1816 and Wordsworth wrote to his friend Coleridge about them in 1799. In 1989 Mark Hamill and Bill Paxton appeared in a film called

Slipstream, which used the falls as a backdrop for a couple of scenes. They also appeared in the 1991 film *Robin Hood: Prince of Thieves* in the scene where Marian (Mary Elizabeth Mastrantonio) comes upon Robin (Kevin Costner) bathing in the pool beneath the falls.

Costner also spent some time in the falls at Aysgarth as they were used for the scene where Robin fights Little John. The falls at the time were extremely dry, with very little water flowing.

AYSGARTH FALLS

The Upper Force of Aysgarth Falls

There are three sections to the waterfall at Aysgarth Falls, the most impressive is probably the Upper Falls, as seen from the parapet of the bridge that carries the road over the River Ure.

The Middle and Lower Falls are accessible on foot using the footpath that also carries the Herriot Way. Viewing platforms have been created for these two sections and the Lower Falls are particularly easy to access.

EAST GILL FORCE
East Gill Force is a two drop waterfall located just outside Keld, where East Gill drops into the River Swale. The upper section is easily spotted beside the path and the Way passes directly over it.

East Gill Force, as it falls into the River Swale

The lower section however, is not so easily seen and a short diversion, along either bank of the Swale, must be taken to get the best view. When the sun is beating down a peaceful, shady spot can be found on the south bank to relax and enjoy the sound of the water.

MILL GILL FORCE

Mill Gill Force is the hidden gem of the Herriot Way. The Way passes close to the falls but there is no marketing of the waterfall by local businesses as there is with Hardraw Force. A short diversion of 50 yards or so, along a sometimes slippery path is required to reach the location, but this is the most rewarding diversion you will take all week.

The diversion is signposted from the path through the woods about ¾ of a mile west of Askrigg. The Herriot Way passes through these woods and the signpost is located right on the path.

When in spate, as seen to the left, the power of the falls is staggering as it erupts from a narrow chute and cascades down the rock face into a curved amphitheatre.

The Lower Force of Aysgarth Falls

HERRIOT WAY WEBSITE

This guide book is supported by a website, which can be found at: **www.herriotway.com**

There is a Downloads section, where you will find GPS waypoints for the Herriot Way. These are free to download and can be imported into many brands of handheld GPS unit.

The website will also be used to identify any errors or amendments to this printed guide, so it may be worth checking this section before you walk. If you find an error in the book, please use this link to report it:
www.herriotway.com/route

Every website address and URL used in this guide is also included in the Links section on the Herriot Way website. This may make it much easier to access the resources described in this book.

Walking the Herriot Way

PART 2 - ROUTE DESCRIPTION

"That quotation about not having time to stand and stare has never applied to me. I seem to have spent a good part of my life - probably too much - in just standing and staring..."

James Herriot, *It Shouldn't Happen to a Vet*

KEY TO VILLAGE SYMBOLS

🛏	B&B/Hotel/Hostel	P	Car Park
🍺	Pub	🍴	Restaurant
🚌	Bus Stop	☎	Phone Box
✚	Chemist	☕	Tea Room
ℹ	TIC Office	🚻	Toilets
✉	Post Office	🛒	Shop
▲	Camp Site	🚶	Outdoor Shop

THE ROUTE

NOTES FROM THE AUTHOR
The notes for the route description are numbered so that you can more easily keep track of where you are on the route, mentally crossing off the numbers as you proceed. Interspersed throughout the narrative you will find 10 digit numbers preceded by two letters; like this (SE 12345 54321). These are Ordnance Survey Grid References and will enable you to check your exact location on the OS map.

I have endeavoured to include every stile, every gate and every turn in the path, but there may be one or two errors along the way. Please feel free to contact me through the website to bring these to my attention and they will be amended for future editions of the guide book.

WALKING TIMES AND DISTANCES
The walking times provided for each section of the walk are estimates only and not based on any scientific formula. Anyone familiar with Naismith's Rule for example, will notice that my estimates assume a much slower walker. Use them as a guide only, your pace will almost certainly be different; such is life.

The simple reason for the difference is that my estimates allow for breaks; quiet moments soaking up a lovely view, pauses for photography, to explore an interesting building, tea breaks, a lunch stop and all the other reasons we decide not to belt along the path at a jog like William W. Naismith obviously did.

Time estimates typically end up being based on my average walking speed of approximately 2 mph, plus a bit of extra time if the section is hilly. Compare that to Naismith's assumption of 3 mph along the flat, plus an extra hour for 2,000 feet of ascent.

The distances for each section and each leg within a section are typically rounded up or down to the nearest ½ mile and the converted kilometres to the nearest integer, which may account for small inaccuracies in the daily mileages. Please forgive me.

SECTION ONE - AYSGARTH TO HAWES
Approx 12 miles (19 km)

The route heads north out of the village, down to the River Ure, which it follows closely along wide meadows and a disused railway track until turning into Askrigg. This is the village that was used to film the James Herriot TV series. From Askrigg the route travels down the Wensleydale valley, through lush green fields, along narrow, secluded lanes to the village of Hardraw with its famous waterfall and then into Hawes, the largest town on the route and the highest market town in Yorkshire.

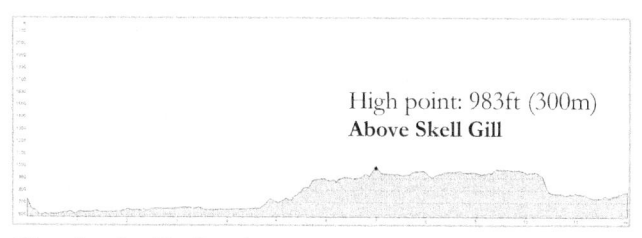

High point: 983ft (300m)
Above Skell Gill

Elevation Profile: Day 1

AYSGARTH

The name Aysgarth comes from old Norse, meaning "the open space in the oak trees". It is situated directly on the A684 and apparently broken into two halves. The houses of the village and one of the pubs are in Aysgarth itself and the parish church and another couple of pubs are located about 1000 yards east along the road. Here they overlook the gorge where the River Ure cascades over Aysgarth Falls - all three of them.

Aysgarth holds one of the most unusual features in any village along the route; its Rock Garden. Aysgarth Rock Garden was commissioned in the first years of the 20th century by Frank Sayer-Graham the then owner of Heather Cottage, which stands opposite. Huge blocks of limestone were brought down from the fells and man-handled into place to create enormous rock- and water-features. Over many years it fell into disrepair but has recently been restored by the present owners and is now open to the public, without charge, during daylight hours.

There are several places to stay in both halves of the village; the **George and Dragon**, **Yoredale Guest House**, **Cornlee Guest House** and **Heather Guest House** are in the western end and **Aysgarth Falls Hotel** and **Wensleydale Farm House** in the eastern end.

The Aysgarth Falls Hotel has a small **campsite**, and another is located at **Colman's of Aysgarth**, beside the George and Dragon, on the A684.

The Aysgarth Falls Hotel serves **bar meals**, as does the George and Dragon pub, which also boasts a **restaurant**.

The Falls Coffee Shop, as its name suggests, is located on the road above the falls, serves hot and cold drinks and food and has a large pay and display **car park** conveniently situated.

Car parking is also possible, but limited, around the village green. This is also used by residents, so check with your B&B that you can leave your car there. Here you will find **Hamilton's Tea Room & Garden**, co-located with Yoredale Guest House, serving the usual fare.

The **National Park Centre** beside Aysgarth Falls, is almost a mile from the village itself. It has ample car parking, a small café and the only **public conveniences**.

There are **bus stops** at both ends of the village. Aysgarth is serviced by bus routes 156 and 157 running between Hawes and Northallerton.

PART 1 - AYSGARTH TO ASKRIGG
Approx 5 miles (8 km) - 2½ to 3 hours

Leaving Aysgarth on the right track is not as easy as it may first appear. There is no "Herriot Way this way" sign and not even a footpath fingerpost to start us on the journey. The surest way to begin is to stand with your back to the war memorial on the green; the wide part of the green ahead, with a bench on the left and Cornlee Guest House facing you. A row of houses lines a narrow tarmac lane on your left. Look for a gap between the houses on your left (SE 00386 88457); opposite the back wall of Cornlee Guest House. This gap leads to an old gate and a fingerpost.

1. Beyond the gate the path turns right and then left descending between trees to a narrow gated stile in a wall. In the field beyond, keep to the wall on our right looking for another narrow gate beneath tall trees.

2. The path continues downhill, on the other side of the wall now, to another narrow gated stile in the wall ahead. Beyond this gate bear right aiming for the corner of the wall and follow it round to the right to another narrow gated stile.

3. Take a sharp left after this gate, still heading downhill through fields, to a narrow gated stile set in a wall beside an old blue gate, beyond this the path descends steeply to a metal gate opening on to a farm yard. This is the old Aysgarth Mill.

4. Turn left along the farm access road and follow this for about 250-300 yards until the lane begin to turn left, uphill. Look for a stile beside a fingerpost (SE 00160 88796), set in the wall ahead of us. Use this to gain access to the field, with the river down to our right.

5. 50 yards after entering the field, we pass a field barn on our right and 50 yards beyond this you will see handles of a ladder stile in the wall on our right. The ladder stile takes us into the woods bordering the River Ure.

6. The path drops down through the woods for a few dozen yards to a slippery and root covered path beside the river and over a wooden stile in a fence into a green pasture. Keep close to the river on our right and follow the path 100 yards around to another wooden stile in a fence.

7. Turn immediately left over the stile and up to meet the road (A684), onto which we turn right. Keep to the right hand side of the road and follow it for about 200-250 yards until we meet what appears to be a lay-by on the right. Leave the road here and cross the Ure on the splendid footbridge provided.

8. Follow the tarmac path on the other side of the bridge as it turns left for about 50-60 yards until it meets a wider track. Look to your left for a fingerpost pointing to a narrow gated stile in the fence (SD 99507 89039) or use the more obvious wide metal gate ahead to enter the same field.

9. Within 50 yards of the gate we cross a narrow beck on concrete stepping stones. The path is now a dark green ribbon against the lighter green of the pasture and hugs the river for about ¼ of a mile until it reaches a fingerpost beside a wall. This confirms we are still on track for Askrigg (and Woodhall).

10. The path is easy on the feet and our green carpet now makes a wide arc beside the river another ¼ of a mile to meet a broken wall coming in from the right.

11. From here we are hemmed in close to the river by the trees and wall on our right, but the path is easy to follow. Flood damage to the bank here forces the path to divert slightly, cutting across the broken wall and then crossing it again a few yards later, to find a gate in a more substantial wall.

12. Beyond this we use duckboards and then a thin gravel path to climb away from the river to meet a field boundary. Initially this is a wire fence, then a sturdy dry stone wall. We pass through a wooden gate, still with the wall on our right, before dropping down and returning to the pasture beside the Ure.

13. Follow the wall (on our right) for about 200 yards until it turns away sharply to the right, we bear right too until we find a fingerpost directing us left, across a culvert in the narrow beck (SD 97707 89706).

14. Keep ahead, with a fence now on our right, aiming for a dry stone wall visible ahead, and the remains of a kissing gate at its end. Beyond the wall, the river swings away left and we stay close to the embankment on our right; the remains of an old railway bed. After 200-300 yards we meet a stile in a fence directly in our path and we use this to climb up to a farm access track with a fingerpost pointing the way to Askrigg.

In 1878 the North Eastern Railway company completed the construction of a railway line between Leyburn and Garsdale Head, providing a rail service to Wensleydale, effectively connecting the Settle Carlisle line to Northallerton. This service ran passenger trains until 1954 and goods trains for a few years more, eventually closing completely in 1959. All that remains are a couple of bridges and the raised rail bed, now used by farmers, sheep and us.

15. At the end of the track go through the gate and keep to the fence on our right for about ¼ of a mile until we reach a narrow footbridge over a beck (SD 96917 90181) and a wall. Beyond the wall keep an eye out for an old metal gate in the hedge on our right. Use this to gain access to the disused railway which we will now use for a while.

16. Turn left onto the disused railway bed and after a couple of hundred yards we will pass beneath a bridge across the path. It can be very wet here, even in a dry period, so make use of the bank on the right of the path to avoid the worst of the mud.

17. Just short of ½ a mile beyond the bridge the path passes through a gate and a few yards later drops off the old railway, to the right and down to a wooden gate beneath the trees.

18. Turn sharp left into the field and follow the fence and then the wall all the way to a large field barn in the corner where we find a stile set high in the wall giving access to a farm road. Don't turn right over the bridge but continue straight ahead down the access road towards the farm buildings ahead. This is Nappa Mill.

19. Turn down the right hand side of the huge green barn, aiming for the gate in the wall and beyond that into the field. The path should be obvious across the field, heading for an incongruous footbridge in the middle of the field. Cross this and then pass through the gate in the wall beyond.

20. Another small footbridge with a gate at each end is crossed (SD 95878 90506) and the path is now close to the Ure again, which we follow for 300-400 yards until reaching a

stile in a wall beside a fingerpost. Join the road, keeping straight ahead, for 50 yards or so, until you see another gated stile and fingerpost leaving the road.

21. Go through this gate and follow the paved path that heads half right across the field. The paving slabs run for about 600 yards in total, firstly through a gate in a wire fence, then shortly after through another in a dry stone wall. In the next field they pass the corner of a wall and eventually terminate at a gate in another wall.

22. Cross the next field and use either the wide gap in the wall ahead, or the pinch stile to its left. Beyond, bear left up the bank passing through the remains of an old metal kissing gate and bear left again.

23. Almost immediately, look for steps and a worn track in the grassy bank on the right, which takes us past another redundant, ancient metal kissing gate and soon leads to a small wooden gate and a wider metal gate beside a wall (SD 95003 90821). Go through this and keep beside the wall on our left.

24. Towards the top of the field, as we approach the houses of the village, the wall bends gently left and at its junction with another wall we use a stone step stile to leave the field. Beyond, keep right and go through a gated stile, keeping to the wall on the right.

25. A few yards and another gated stile is located beneath a tall tree which leads up to another wooden gated stile. Go through this, across the grass and along the drive between the houses, to emerge into the lovely village of Askrigg.

26. Turn right along the road. The church of St. Oswald is on our left and Sykes Store and Tea Room on our right.

ASKRIGG

Askrigg is the home, to a generation of TV fans at least, of James Herriot. The filming of the long-running BBC TV series was based in Askrigg. Skeldale House, the home of the veterinary practice was located in a building which has subsequently been renamed to Skeldale House. The name

Askrigg is derived from the Old Norse meaning "the ridge where Ash trees grow".

There are several places to find a bed in Askrigg, there are three B&Bs just off the market place; **Manor House**, **The Apothecary's House** and **Holmedale** and beds are also available in the **White Rose Hotel**.

There are three pubs in the village; the **Kings Arms**, the **White Rose Hotel** and the **Crown Inn**, all located just off the market place, on the main road heading north east.

Sykes Country Store is the only general store in the village and also houses one of the two Tea Rooms. It's open every day, quite early and stocks the usual general store merchandise.

Parking is available in the market place and there is an honesty box system in place, located on the wall outside the church. This gets very busy though and will be full unless you're early or lucky. An additional small car park is provided at the north eastern end of the village.

A **telephone box** is located in the market place, in front of the church and opposite our entry into the village and the shop.

There are two **tea rooms** in the village; the **Humble Pie** which is open every day except Sunday and the **Sykes Tea Room** which is open every day. A **public convenience** is located in the Temperance Hall towards the southern end of the village, only 100 yards or so from the market place.

There is a **bus stop** in the market place. Askrigg is serviced by bus routes 156 and 157 running between Hawes and Northallerton.

All manner of temptations are available here and it's perfectly situated for lunch, being just short of halfway between Aysgarth and Hawes. If the weather is nice however, consider buying picnic items and carrying them to Mill Gill Force, just a little further along the Way.

Note: "Gill" or "Ghyll" is a local word for ravine or stream, derived from the Old Norse term "gil" with the same meaning.

PART 2 - ASKRIGG TO SEDBUSK
Approx 4½ miles (7 km) - 2½ hours

1. We leave Askrigg along the little lane to the right of the old market cross (SD 94804 91045), outside the church, appropriately named Church View and follow this as it winds between houses for about 300-400 yards.

2. After the last of the houses on the right, look out for a narrow gate (possibly the narrowest gate ever) beside a much larger gate with a fingerpost pointing to "Mill Gill Falls ½ml". The path beyond is paved all the way to the opposite wall where is drops down through a stile and around the disused West Saw Mill. The path passes beneath an elevated zinc pentrough that used to feed the mill.

3. Follow the fingerpost pointing right as the wooded path now runs beside the river again and down to a narrow wooden footbridge. Cross the bridge and climb the steps on the other side to a narrow gated stile where we turn sharp right and through another gated stile into more woods.

4. The path climbs through the woods, closely bordered by the wall on the left and trees on the right, several times we need to squeeze past large trees that encroach on the path. Follow the obvious path for about 400-500 yards.

5. Here we meet a fork in the path and a low fingerpost (SD 93870 91379). The right fork takes us to "Mill Gill Fall Only" and the left fork takes us along the Herriot Way.

Turn right at the junction and follow the narrow path as it drops gently and soon arrives at Mill Gill Force; another splendid waterfall that spills its contents through a narrow rock chute down to the rocks below. When it's in spate this waterfall is even more impressive than Hardraw Force. Well worth the short diversion.

---

6. Follow the sign for "Whitfield Gill" and continue to climb up through the woods for another 100 yards or so over tree roots and smooth stones to a large multi-fingerpost at a junction of paths. We leave the woods here, following

the "Public Footpath Helm" finger over a narrow gated stile into the field beyond.

7. The path is beside the wall in this field, passing a field barn and a strange sign that proclaims the "footpath was legally closed in 1986" to a narrow gated stile in a wall. About 200 yards beyond this stile the wall ends and we continue straight ahead, using a four-wheel drive track to travel the remaining few yards to a wide vehicle gate. There is a stile in the wall beside the gate, but either way we join the road.

8. Turn left onto the road and then immediately right at the junction to join the minor road that will take us to Skell Gill. At just under ¾ of a mile, this is the longest section of road walking we have to do on the Herriot Way and even this length can be interrupted with a visit to a restored Lime Kiln.

9. Look out for a gate on the left 200 yards or so after joining the road (SD 93108 91482), a sign announces "Grange Gill Lime Kiln" and it's worth the diversion if only to walk on the lush grass instead of the tarmac road. A path climbing up beyond the lime kiln will return us to the road after our visit, so there's no need to retrace steps.

10. Back on the road and we soon cross a bridge over Dumbha Gill. A few more minutes and we pass a farm and some holiday rentals into the lovely hamlet of Skell Gill. Cross the hump-back bridge and follow the narrow walled lane for another 200-300 yards, the tarmac giving out to a grassy strip between ruts. The track eventually runs into a ford, but just before this there is a junction to the left (SD 92172 91499), which is where we want to go. The fingerpost at the junction says "Sedbusk 2½ ml". Turn left.

11. The rutted track continues between walls and climbs gently to a pair of gates, where the lane ends. Continuing into the field beyond, the path runs past a field barn and uphill more steeply, but still beside the wall.

12. Almost at the top of the hill we meet another fingerpost; the "Sedbusk" finger points us away from the wall and across the open field, still with a short climb to complete,

Section One - Aysgarth to Hawes

before we drop down the other side, where we meet another wall.

13. A hundred or so yards after joining this new wall we pass through a wide metal gate and 100 yards or so further on we pass a fingerpost and a farmhouse with dozens of newly planted trees opposite it (replacing the recently felled mature plantation that used to be here).

14. Stay with the wall and we soon pass through another gate and 100 yards beyond that is another farmhouse with wide metal gates just before it and just after it. This is Shaw Cote on the Ordnance Survey map (SD 91134 90955).

15. A further 200 yards and we come to another gate and another farm property. The owners have created a permissive path that bypasses the farm's yards using a path to the right. It is well signed and easy to follow and avoids all the usual potential problems of dogs, machinery and livestock. The path passes through a couple of narrow gates, over a tiny footbridge, through another narrow wooden gate and then through a narrow gated stile in the wall, to exit the farm area.

16. Follow the fence beyond the last gate to reach a four-wheel drive track that runs for 100 yards or so to a wide vehicle gate. The track continues for another 200 yards or so until it reaches another wide vehicle gate where it becomes a green lane.

17. The green lane passes a field barn after a few dozen yards and then goes through a wide metal gate into a narrow lane between walls. After 100 yards the lane begins to turn away to the left, but we leave it here using a wide metal gate on the right (SD 90239 90963), or the stone stile beside it.

18. The field we enter is rough grazing land and can be quite boggy. To avoid the worst of the mud, stick close to the wall on our left until you see a green trod between the tall grasses. This takes us over the tiny Nicholl Gill, using a stone step and almost immediately through a narrow gated stile in a wall.

19. Another 100 yards and we pass through another gated stile, the green path still running between tall marsh grass

and up to another narrow gated stile. Here we leave the rough grazing behind and enter rich green pastures. The path now running beside a wall to our right.

20. The next stile is set up in the wall and 100 yards beyond that we reach another stile which takes us out of the fields and onto an access road for the buildings at Litherskew. Turn right beyond the stile and follow the access road for about 20 yards.

The OS map appears to be out of date at this point, suggesting the footpath runs up and around the back of the houses further up the hill, but this is not the case. Follow the notes below.

---

21. You will see a fingerpost beside the track on the right. It guides us left down the back of the building on our left and then past another house on our right. Be brazen! This is the public Right of Way and the occupiers are well used to folk wandering past their front window.

22. After passing the house and their garage on the right, use a gated stile set in the stone wall, beside what could be the front door of the house. This stile gives out onto the fields again.

23. The path across the fields is obvious, even if it weren't for the gated stiles in the walls ahead to aim for. 50-60 yards beyond Litherskew we pass through one of these and 100 yards later we pass through another.

24. The next gate is set beside a small conifer plantation (SD 89198 91087) and the one after that is set high in the dry stone wall with steps up to it.

25. Within 100 yards we pass through an open gateway (with a stile set in the wall beside it) and directly beyond that is a narrow gated stile in the wall. You will now see the path running ahead into a plantation of mainly deciduous trees. Use the stile in the wall to enter the trees and the path within to reach another gated stone stile with a sheep creep beside it.

26. The path now runs beside the wall on our right, 100 yards or so to another narrow gated stile in a wall, passing a row of houses on the right and reaching the road into Sedbusk.

Turn right along the road and up to the tiny village green, opposite a telephone box.

SEDBUSK

Really nothing more than a cluster of houses, Sedbusk offers the walker no convenience other than a bench to sit on if the sun is shining and a **telephone box** to shelter in if it's pelting down. Even the narrow road through the village is a dead-end for vehicles.

PART 3 - SEDBUSK TO HAWES

Approx 2½ miles (4 km) - 1 to 1½ hours (this does not include any time spent visiting Hardraw Force)

1. The village green has to be the smallest of any we will find on the Herriot Way, but it is tidy, well maintained and offers the comfort of a bench for weary walkers. Just to the right of the bench is a gap in the low wall, with a fingerpost (SD 88314 91210) pointing us to Simonstone, just visible through the lichen. This leads to a narrow passage between two houses and out to a gated stile beyond.

2. For the next ¾ of a mile the path cuts across sixteen narrow fields, each one with a small gated stile in it, or perhaps a larger traditional gate. For those that wish to count them down the series that follows the gate above is;

    Narrow gate, narrow gate, narrow gate, narrow stile, narrow gate, narrow gate beside large gate, narrow gate beside large gate, narrow gate beside large gate, narrow gate beside barn, narrow gate, narrow gate beside large gate.

3. After that final narrow gate, located beside a wider vehicle gate and both next to a stone field barn, the track crosses a field and reaches a farm entrance. The wide gate into the yard leads to a pair of ladder stiles in quick succession over farm walls. These are two of the trickiest ladder stiles you'll encounter on the walk; take care, especially when they're wet.

4. We exit the farm on a concrete access road, passing through a wide metal gate and continuing for a few more yards until we reach the road.

5. Turn left onto the road, cross to the other side and turn right into a wide drive (SD 87243 91467), following a fingerpost that says "FP Hardraw ¼". The drive bends left and then right and after a hundred yards or so arrives at the impressive facade of Simonstone Hall.

SIMONSTONE

Simonstone itself is located ¼ of a mile north of the Herriot Way path, just north of Hardraw, but the Way runs along the drive of the Simonstone Hotel, the only notable building in the village and now famous for the "Top Gear Fracas".

The **Simonstone Hotel** is the only B&B accommodation available. It also serves **drinks**, both alcoholic and **teas** and coffees and has a **restaurant** that is open to non-residents

6. Just before we turn right into the entrance of the hall, look for a narrow stile in the wall on our left, gated as usual. This is perhaps the narrowest stile of the day so far! It gives on to a short flight of steps which drop down into a field. Follow the wall on our right for a hundred yards or so to another narrow gated stile.

7. The path beyond should be clear; a dark green stripe across the lighter green of the field, leading to a cluster of farm buildings. On the other side of the yard is a wide vehicle gate beside a narrow gated stile in the wall. Go through this and turn left (south west) down the hill to a flight of steep stone steps (SD 86927 91402) leading to a more traditional wooden stile over a fence. The village of Hardraw can be seen below.

8. The wooden stile leads to a few more stone steps and then to a steep, cobbled path down the field. After a hundred yards or so this meets a wall and then a wooden kissing gate into someone's back garden! This is a public Right of Way however. The path then drops through a stone stile

into their front yard and we exit with some relief into the street.

HARDRAW

Hardraw, or possibly Hardrow if some of the local footpath signs are to be believed, has become famous for (and possibly owes its existence to) the waterfall; Hardraw Force. The water spills from Hardraw Beck and drops almost 100 feet into a wide amphitheatre below. Tourists have been visiting the spot since the 18th century which is located in the grounds of the Green Dragon Inn. A small fee is payable to the owners, as has always been the case, and the path behind the pub leads down to this stunning waterfall. If you've been cursed by rain on your Herriot Way walk, then here is the upside - the waterfall is absolutely spectacular after heavy rain.

The **Green Dragon Inn** controls access to the waterfall and provides bar meals and accommodation. The **Hardraw Old School Bunkhouse** provides the only other accommodation before we reach Hawes.

Parking is limited in the village. There is room for perhaps half a dozen cars by the roadside at the western edge of the village. An honesty box system is in place. There is a **telephone box** opposite the pub, right on the Herriot Way path.

The **Cart House Tea Room** serves hot and cold refreshments and a selection of handmade craft items. It's located on the other side of the bridge from the Inn.

A **bus stop** is located opposite the pub, serviced by the Little White Bus which will take you to Garsdale station or Hawes.

9. To our right is the Green Dragon Inn, home to Hardraw Force, England's tallest, above ground, single drop waterfall, where the water spills 98 feet from top to bottom.

After paying a small entrance fee in their Visitor Centre, you can take a stroll down the path, through the trees to visit Hardraw Force. This is best seen after recent rains when a torrent of water spills over the rocky lip into a large stone amphitheatre. Turner painted this site in about 1816 and Wordsworth mentioned it in one of his letters in 1799. In the past you used to be able to walk behind the waterfall, but this is no longer easy, advisable or allowed. Hollywood actors Kevin Costner (in *Robin Hood Prince of Thieves*) and Mark Hamill (in *Slipstream*) have both done just this though. Hardraw Force is a popular setting for movies.

10. Directly opposite the pub is a telephone box and a Pennine Way sign, we will be using the UK's first National Trail to reach Hawes, so navigation from here should be aided considerably by the fingerposts.

11. Go down the drive opposite the pub, with the telephone box on our right, to reach a kissing gate which provides access to a field with a path that runs alongside the wall on our left. The path is paved to prevent erosion from the thousands of pairs of boots that use it every year.

12. The path reaches another kissing gate, another few dozen yards of paved path and another gate beyond. The paved path becomes a little broken as it passes to the right of a large mound with a tree on it, but after 150 yards it reaches a narrow gated stile in a wall.

13. A further hundred yards and we reach a wooden gate, beside a larger vehicle gate, either of which gives on to a wide field with another hundred yards or so of paved footpath.

14. The paved path ends at the next wall with another wooden gate beside a wider gate. The path forks here (SD 87157 90934), but ideally we should keep to the left. The right fork brings us out at almost exactly the same spot, but the path is lower and runs through a meadow prone to flooding, so if there has been any rain recently it will be very wet underfoot. The left fork keeps to a higher route and is dry all year round.

15. The grassy path of the left fork runs for about 100 yards to a kissing gate and beyond this it follows the line of some overhead cables for another 150 yards to another kissing gate. Keep close to the wall to our right in the next field and you can look down to the lower path. Smile with self-

satisfaction if the ladder stile is surrounded by a large pool of water. Pass a stone bench that looks out over the fields and the loops of the River Ure and less than 100 yards further on we come to a gated stile that drops down to a road.

16. Turn right onto the road and follow it as it drops gently downhill, following a bend in the Ure before crossing the river on a wide bridge. On the other side, set into the stone wall is a gap stile that provides access to a path running beside the road; a safer option than walking along the road itself.

17. After a few yards the path re-joins the road we need to aim for a gate in the wall on the opposite side of the road, with a Pennine Way fingerpost beside it (SD 87588 90255). Climb the few steps beyond and follow the paved path through the field about 150 yards to a kissing gate.

18. We are back at the road again. Turn left through the gate and then right at the T-junction using the pavement beside the road as it climbs gently towards Hawes. Keep an eye out on the left, at the top of the rise, for the old steam engine stranded on a few feet of line beside the Dales Countryside Museum. A path gives access to the train and the museum if you have time and the inclination.

19. If not, continue along the road for another 100 yards until we reach a major road intersection, where you will find a small green enclosure in the middle. A wooden shepherd and his wooden dog round up a flock of wooden sheep in this fenced-off space. Take either of the roads on the right to reach the centre of Hawes. A veritable oasis of shops, tea rooms and pubs.

HAWES

Hawes is the largest town on the Herriot Way and is also the highest market town in England at 850 feet above sea level. The town dates back as far as the 14th century and is now filled with shops, cafes and pubs. Market day is Tuesday and the town becomes a busy, bustling place as it fills with folk from all around. If you are interested in local crafts then a visit to the

Wensleydale Creamery and the **Ropemaker** should be included on your itinerary; the former shows the production of the world-famous cheese and the latter the production of ropes, both provide an interesting diversion.

There are numerous B&Bs, pubs and hotels in the town, as well as the Youth Hostel. You will have no problem finding just the type of accommodation you need in Hawes. These include; **Spring Bank House**, **Cockett's Hotel**, **Loxley House** and several pubs in the centre of the village as well as **Herriot's Guest House** and **Laburnum House** which both offer additional refreshments as well. The **Old Station House** is located by the Dales Museum.

There are several pubs on the main street including the **Old Board Inn**, the **Crown**, the **Fountain**, the **Bulls Head** and the **White Hart Inn**. All the pubs serve food.

Hawes has plenty of **car parking**, both along the main street if you arrive early enough and in **two car parks**, one at each end of the village. Charges are payable for parking, but as with all Yorkshire Dales car parks, these are quite reasonable.

There are two **telephone boxes** in the town; one on the main street opposite the Old Board Inn and one on the other side of the town, on the northern side of the "loop" on the bridge over the river.

Hawes is well stocked with **tea rooms**; **Penny Garth Café** and **Laburnum House Tea Room** are both on the main street. **Herriot's Gallery** also has a tea room, further down the street.

Some shops in the town will provide cash-back on purchases. More importantly, however, there is a branch of **Barclays Bank** with a **cash machine** outside.

There are **bus stops** in the main street and another situated at the Dales Museum. Hawes is serviced by a number of different services including the 156 to Leyburn, which calls at Askrigg and Aysgarth.

A **Tourist Information Centre** is located at the **Dales Countryside Museum**, next to the long silent steam engine, still waiting patiently by the platform at the old Hawes station.

The **public library** in Hawes has facilities for Internet and email. It's located down a side street, off the main street, between **The Bay Tree Bistro** and the Bulls Head. It's only open on weekdays though and closes at about 16:30, with an evening opening on a Thursday for a couple of hours.

The **Spar shop** (a small supermarket) is located on the main street and is open from 08:00 to 18:00 weekdays and slightly amended versions of these at weekends. The **Old Sweet Shop** sells both sweets and tobacco, which is novel. There are **two outdoor shops** in the town; one on the main street and another further down by the river. **Elijah Allen stocks groceries** and other provisions.

A **Post Office**; open 09:00 to 17:30 Monday to Saturday (closed on Sunday) is situated in the Community Office just off the main street, between the Bulls Head and The Bay Tree café.

Wensleydale Panty, **The Chippie Hawes** which as well as doing excellent take-away also has a cafe attached, Penny Garth Café does many things well, including Pizza and along with Cockett's Restaurant, is on the main street. The Bay Tree cafe and bistro is hidden away next to the Bulls Head. Caffe Curva is a cheerful place serving hot drinks and snacks.

John Hogg's chemist (or pharmacy) is situated on the main street, it also serves wines and spirits, which is another novel combination.

SECTION TWO - HAWES TO KELD
Approx 12½ miles (20 km)

Leaving Hawes, the Way climbs up the side of Great Shunner Fell, the third highest mountain in Yorkshire, following the mostly paved footpath of the Pennine Way, to the summit shelter with wide-ranging views across the surrounding dales and hills and then down into Thwaite. From here the path skirts the lower slopes of Kisdon and then drops down again into the tiny settlement of Keld.

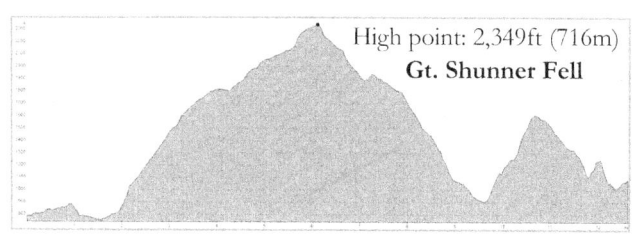

High point: 2,349ft (716m)
Gt. Shunner Fell

Elevation Profile: Day 2

PART 1 - HAWES TO GREAT SHUNNER FELL
Approx 6 miles (10 km) - 3½ to 4 hours

1. We exit Hawes at the opposite end of the village from the one we entered it. If you stayed at the Youth Hostel then you're perfectly positioned. Take the A684 out of the village (signposted Sedbergh and Kirkby Stephen) and follow it downhill for 200 yards or so.

2. As we approach the Ashes, with its large, walled turning circle on the right hand side of the road, look for a fingerpost and a walled lane on the left hand side, leaving the A684 (SD 86680 90031). This takes us uphill towards farm buildings.

3. Towards the top of the lane, keep to the right fork and pass through a wide metal gate in a wall and another identical gate, almost immediately in a fence, passing into the fields. Keep to the left of the field and aim for the stand of trees directly ahead. There is a wall here and a stile which leads us into another field.

4. Cross a tiny stream and continue beside the wall on our left heading for a narrow gated stile in the wall ahead, beneath a tree. This gives onto a field, which we ascend, aiming for the barn a hundred yards or so ahead.

5. To the left of the barn is a gate and a tree and a narrow stile in the wall, use this to cross the wall and then head half right (north west) across the field. After 100 yards we arrive at a wide wooden gate in a wall. We may have the benefit of a green track through the next field; if not, look for a post ahead to guide us over the hill.

6. At the crest you can look ahead; the next half a dozen miles or so of our route are visible, the green hump of Great Shunner Fell dominating the skyline. Use the guide post on the descending slope to reach a narrow gated stile in the next wall. A final post leads us down to the path beside the old railway embankment. Head left to find a gate and stile (SD 85665 90358) which give on to a tarmac road passing under the arch of the huge viaduct.

7. Turn right (north) onto the road and follow it for perhaps 200 yards, beside Widdale Beck, until it reaches another road, the A684 which we left a few minutes ago. Turn left over the bridge, after a few yards we pass a farm entrance on the left and a few yards beyond is another one. Look for a stile set in the wall beside this second farm entrance.

8. Use the stile and turn immediately right, following the wall and walking parallel with the A684. After a hundred yards or so, we pass through a narrow gate in a wall and then immediately cross a narrow footbridge. The wall on our right now becomes a fence and a few yards later, just as we reach the parapet of the road bridge, we use a ladder stile to climb up onto the road.

9. Turn left onto the road and cross New Bridge, following the road for a short way as it bends left and reaches a junction.

10. Turn right here, almost as if we were taking the road to Hardraw, but look for a fingerpost and a narrow gated stile in the wall on the other side of the road. Use the stile to gain access to the field beside the road. The green path

should be fairly obvious across the field, straight ahead, passing a power pole on our right, to reach a wider gate in the far wall.

11. Beyond this gate the path crosses the tiny waterway of Broad Carr Sike and heads half left uphill to another gate. We are leaving the lush green pastures of the lowlands now and the grasses become rougher and taller as we climb gently. Use the guide posts (not always easy to spot) to contour around the lower slopes of Bluebell Hill. Looking ahead you will be able to see the posts dropping down the other side of the hill and then crossing a narrow gulley, before climbing again to meet a wall with a ladder stile. Once you drop down into the gulley it's not easy to identify the best ascent route to the ladder stile, so it's worth picking your spot now, while you can.

12. In the bottom of the gulley is a fingerpost (SD 85807 91611). The finger pointing in our direction of travel should help you spot the handles of the ladder stile we are aiming for, just to the right of a small wind-bent tree. Climb the steep grassy slope to the stile.

13. Use the ladder stile to gain access to a very rough field and follow the wall on our right as it climbs uphill until we reach a gate in the wall at the top of the field.

14. The gate gives on to a narrow walled lane, onto which we turn left and climb a short distance, only a couple of hundred yards, to a dry stone wall across the path with a pair of wide vehicle gates and a ladder stile giving access to the open fell beyond.

15. Almost immediately the four-wheel drive track splits; we go left as directed by the Pennine Way fingerpost (SD 85763 92129) while the right track heads along the old Hearne Coal Road to Pickersett Nab.

16. The path climbs steadily now and views open up to the left and right. After about ½ a mile the path meets a dry stone wall for a short distance before that runs off to the left. 200-300 yards after the brief encounter with the wall, we pass an old quarry and spoil heap on the left of the path.

17. The path now describes an S bend, up to and around the limestone crags of Hearne Top and a couple of hundred yards beyond that we come to another gate in a wall, this one also has a ladder stile beside it. The four-wheel drive track continues through the gate and continues to climb for a few dozen yards before it meets another Pennine Way fingerpost (SD 84686 93242).

18. Bear right here, along the Pennine Way, onto a less well defined path; obviously still used by farm vehicles, but not as compacted underfoot. From this point the path is partly paved and partly across natural gritstone outcrops. There are some parts of the path where erosion has led to a myriad of thin paths through the heather or across grassy sections but following the route should be simple, even in bad weather. There are many cairns beside the path as well, and these will keep us true on a misty ascent.

Note: A cairn is a pile of stones, often just loosely piled, sometimes constructed into a pillar or pyramid, used for guidance by shepherds and travellers.

The paving stones are laid to prevent the erosion of the peat, rather than assist walkers. The result however is a much easier surface to walk on. Although many people don't like the slabs the alternative is a landscape scarred by dozens of parallel paths created by people trying to avoid previously eroded and boggy routes. Many of the slabs were reclaimed from the floors of redundant mills and you will see holes drilled in some of them where machinery was fixed to the floor.

---

19. The ascent of Great Shunner Fell is fairly unremarkable. Keep an eye open for the various cairns, pillars and beacons that litter the lower slopes - you should be able to see about half a dozen without leaving the path. On clear days the views during the ascent are fantastic.

The path can become very wet and boggy after persistent rain, even the paving stones will be under two or three inches of water in places.

---

20. There are several false summits on the ascent, especially in poor visibility; be prepared for at least two and allow two

hours for the ascent from the road and you won't be too far off. The path eventually meets a fence line with a stile and the structure you can see beyond that is the summit shelter. Cross the stile and take a well-earned rest; it's all downhill to Thwaite from here.... well, almost.

Part 2 - Great Shunner Fell to Thwaite
Approx 3½ miles (6 km) - 1½ to 2 hours

1. The summit shelter (SD 84861 97277) is cross-shaped, providing shelter from any wind direction. It's a comfortable spot for lunch and incorporates the OS triangulation pillar (or trig point) in its north eastern edge.

2. After admiring the views, follow the path away from the shelter (north east) a few yards to another fence line with a gate in it.

3. The path is mostly paved for the next three miles or so, although there are some sections that take advantage of gritstone outcrops and other stable surfaces to avoid the need for paving. Even in poor weather the path is easy to follow, there are no diversions and no points where it disappears completely and in clear weather you can see the path ahead for a good distance.

4. The paving stones eventually peter out just short of a gate in a wall (SD 87580 98437) at the head of a very rough four-wheel drive track that runs between dry stone walls. Go through the gate and follow the track as it descends steadily over stones and cobbles and then over packed sand for about a mile until it reaches a road and another Pennine Way fingerpost (SD 88950 98357). The hill directly ahead is Kisdon, our next destination.

5. Turn right (south east) onto the road and follow it for a couple of hundred yards until it reaches the village of Thwaite on the B6270. Thwaite is a little gold-mine for the weary (and possibly wet) walker who has just traversed one of the biggest hills in Yorkshire.

THWAITE

The name "Thwaite", like so many local names, has its roots in Old Norse; originally a "thveit" was a clearing, which suggests much of the surrounding area used to be woodland or forested. The bulk of Great Shunner Fell stands guard over little Thwaite and this is also a derivation from Old Norse, where a "sjonar" meant a look out hill. Perhaps in the 9th and 10th centuries the hill wasn't clad in low cloud or mist as often as it is nowadays.

Thwaite is a lovely little hamlet in just the right location and with just the right amount of conveniences to make it a "must do" stop along the route. If you're walking anti-clockwise, it's far enough from Keld for morning tea and if you're coming in the other direction, far enough from Hawes for a late lunch.

Other than holiday cottages (multi-day, self-catering accommodation) the only beds available in Thwaite are at the **Kearton Country Hotel**. They provide Dinner, Bed & Breakfast rates for one night or multiple nights.

They also run the **Kearton Tea Shop**, situated next to the Hotel and serving teas, coffees, lunches and snacks. It's also a craft shop selling locally made items and has postcards and souvenirs for sale too.

The **telephone box** is located on the B6270, hidden from view around the back of the building holding the Parish Notice Board and a sign for the Kearton County Hotel. There is no mobile reception in the village on any network.

The **bus stop** is located on the B6270, beside the telephone box. Thwaite is serviced by the 30, 36 and 480R routes running between Richmond and Keld.

PART 3 - THWAITE TO KELD
Approx 3 miles (5 km) - 1½ to 2 hours

1. Continue on through Thwaite village with the Tea Shop and pub on your left and head for a cottage at the end of the lane, just to the right of a gated farm yard. The cottage has a Pennine Way fingerpost (SD 89275 98199) and a lamp post in front of it. Our path uses a stile built into the

garden wall of the cottage to access a path to its left. Climb up through the stile and turn right, down the side of the building along a narrow path between stone walls to a gate with another narrow gate just beyond it.

2. Pass through the gate and follow the path beside the wall to another narrow gate about 50 yards ahead with a Pennine Way fingerpost beside it. The fingerpost points us through the gate and then left across the field, telling us we are 3 miles from Keld.

If you're heading for Usha Gap Campsite or lodgings in Muker tonight and not Keld, then jump to Part 3a on page 75 and continue reading from there.

3. The path across the field runs to a gate and then beyond that to another gate across a narrow stream. Turn right after passing through the gate and walk beside the stream towards a dry stone wall where the path turns left (north east), in front of the wall, and climbs the hill with the wall to our right.

4. At the top of the field there is a narrow gate protecting a pinch stile in the dry stone wall, which gives on to the bracken-covered hillside beyond. A narrow, rocky path climbs up through the bracken, passing a couple of large cairns before the bracken fades and the path reaches a wall. We follow the wall for a few dozen yards before the path strikes out, up the face of the hill again reaching another gated stile in a wall.

5. The path beyond is fairly obvious and runs towards a wall corner slightly up and to the right of our position at the stile. Follow the path as it reaches the wall and then turns left, between a small stone barn and a lone tree to another gate 50 yards or so ahead (SD 90097 98472).

6. Go through this gate and bear right, uphill slightly, towards a fingerpost at a turn in the wall. We turn sharp right (east) with the wall here, following the Pennine Way still, towards a house about 100 yards or so from the fingerpost.

7. Keep the house to our right and at its far end is a field gate, which we go through, immediately followed by another field gate slightly to our left, with a Pennine Way fingerpost sandwiched between the two. This second gate takes us steeply uphill on a grassy track between stone walls about 150 yards to another Pennine Way fingerpost opposite a low-roofed stone barn.

8. Here we bid farewell to the Pennine Way (for a while) as it continues straight ahead, while we turn sharp left (north) putting the low-roofed barn at our backs and keeping the stone wall close to our left as we climb steeply uphill.

9. Keeping the dry stone wall to our left, climb uphill. The green track we are using soon picks up another wall on our right and after about 200 yards it meets a gate. You've probably already been admiring the views to the right, down into Swaledale; surely one of the loveliest of all the Yorkshire Dales?

10. Beyond this gate the track leaves the walls behind and after a few yards appears to split in two; one green track keeping to the right beside the wall and one heading left uphill between two green embankments. Either path will do - they both meet up again in a minute. The path to the right provides great views up the valley towards Swinner Gill, where we will be walking tomorrow and across to valley to Black Hill and Ivelet Side above Muker.

11. The two paths meet again in front of a dry stone wall, which we turn left along for a short distance until we reach a gate (SD 90072 99047) which gives on to open moorland and a green path through the coarse grass either side. The path soon begins to descend gradually.

12. After perhaps 400-500 yards the path arrives at another gate in a dry stone wall and beyond this the path runs gently downhill between a pair of broken stone walls, about 150 yards to another gate.

13. Continue through, almost straight ahead, down the hill, about 100 yards to another gate with a fingerpost beside it. Follow the direction of the finger towards Keld; that is through the gate and along the rabbit-cropped grass path,

obvious as it cuts through the rough moorland grass on either side.

14. This section of the path allows us retrospective views of Great Shunner Fell over our left shoulder, but focussing ahead again we follow the path for about 400-500 yards until we reach another gate. Beyond this, aim for the corner of the wall about 100 yards ahead.

15. At the wall corner (SD 89402 99959) an access road bends right to reach the farmhouse, but our track runs to the left of the wall down to yet another gate about 100 yards further on. From here the path begins to descend a little more steeply as we lose the height we gained on the ascent of Kisdon.

16. Our grassy path has now become a rugged four-wheel drive track, descending steeply with the hillside to our left dropping off to the valley below. The track soon arrives at another gate which leads onto a lane lined, firstly on the left and then on both sides, by old, moss-covered stone walls and a line of trees.

17. The lane bends left after 100 yards or so and drops down to a gate at a shallow ford, with a concrete footbridge to one side for pedestrians. Follow the lane for another 100 yards, past an old field barn up to the B6270 road.

If you didn't manage to secure accommodation in Keld itself and you are staying at **Greenlands B&B** you need to turn left along the road here, for about ½ a mile, returning back to this point tomorrow morning to continue.

18. Turn right onto the road (NY 89215 00602) and within ¼ of a mile we arrive at the tiny village of Keld.

As we approach the village, look for the war memorial in the wall beside the road, commemorating four men that died in the "Great War". Four men from such a small community perhaps indicates the scale of the losses suffered in that conflict.

Section Two - Hawes to Keld 73

KELD

Keld is more a cluster of buildings, a hamlet maybe, rather than a village. However, in terms of amenities it punches well above its weight; offering a tea room, a pub and public toilets where other much larger settlements have none of these. The most likely reason for this is its importance as a crossroad on two of the most popular long distance paths in the UK; the Pennine Way and Wainwright's Coast to Coast.

There is some evidence of buildings in Keld dating back as far as the 17th century, with a barn in the field just to the east of the village sporting a 1687 datestone above its doorway. Park Lodge has an original datestone from 1760 and out-buildings that were added in each successive century.

The two chapels in the village and many of the other buildings sprang from the prosperity of the lead mining industry in the mid-19th century. Once this died away however, the village seems to have been forgotten as there is very little 20th century influence; probably not a bad thing at all.

There are relatively few B&Bs in Keld, in comparison to the number of walkers that use the village. **Butt House B&B** is the large farmhouse by the telephone box at the top of the village, close to the old Youth Hostel, which is now a hotel called **Keld Lodge**, which offers food and drink as well as rooms. **East View B&B**, in the heart of the village has rooms.

Keld Lodge also serves food to non-residents with an interesting menu and fantastic views from the large picture windows. **Butt House** provides an evening meal for residents as does **East View**.

Ample **car parking** is available at the bottom end of the village, furthest from the main road, in the yard of **Park Lodge Farm**. They charge a small fee and ask that you use the honesty box by the entrance of the car park to deposit your coins. Enquire in the shop for longer stays.

A **telephone box** is located on the edge of the village, between Keld Lodge and Butt House. There is no mobile reception in the village on any network.

Keld Public Hall, at the bottom of the village, close to where our path arrives, has a community run **tea room** in the winter, that provides hot and cold drinks, a selection of locally made cakes and other supplies most welcome at the end of a long walk. There's plenty of seating in the hall, if it's raining.

The **bus stop** is located on the B6270 beside the telephone box, just down from Keld Lodge. Keld is serviced by the following bus routes; 30, 36 and 480R running to Richmond.

PART 3A - THWAITE TO MUKER
Approx 1½ miles (2 km) - 45 mins to 1 hour

1. Our path to Muker lies directly ahead while the path to Keld turns left and heads up over Kisdon Hill. Follow the path on the lip of the steep bank of the river to our right.

2. For the next 300-400 yards the path uses narrow gaps in the field walls to make progress across the hay meadows. These fields form an important part of the summer grazing for the sheep and as the local farmer is keen on telling us; we should keep to single file through these.

3. Just beyond the first narrow gated stile since leaving Thwaite we find a tiny cobbled bridge over the beck. Use this and follow the path to another gated stile in the wall ahead. Go through this and turn sharp right alongside the wall.

4. Several more narrow fields follow, with the path passing a large barn and then running between a wall on our left and the beck on our right, before meeting the road at Usha Gap Bridge.

5. We don't cross the bridge but continue straight ahead along the road for 50-60 yards until we reach the entrance to **Usha Gap Farm**. They run a large campsite in the field beside the road and in the field behind the farm buildings.

6. Turn into the farm entrance, even if you're not camping, and bear right through the yard and into a field beyond.

Head half left through the field, looking for a narrow gated stile in the stone wall (SD 90285 98047). This is not easy to spot, but it stands between two wide metal stock gates you can see in the wall ahead, very close to the gate further away.

7. Go through this little gated stile and follow the wall. 300-400 yards and several more narrow stiles later, the path meets a set of overhead cables. It roughly follows these for another 400-500 yards, through several more narrow stiles until it reaches the village of Muker.

8. We enter the village through a wide wooden gate (or the narrow gap beside it). Looking down to your right you can see the tops of the houses of the village.

9. Beyond the gate, turn right down a steep, narrow track beside a curving stone wall. This leads down to the road and emerges in front of the Farmers Arms pub.

MUKER

Muker gets its name from Old Norse - in this case "Mjor-aker" or narrow acre. The Vikings farmed the area and this remained the major activity until the 1800s when lead mining became prevalent. Like Keld, just up the valley, Muker was a hub of mining activity. Upon its decline, farming took over again and now tourism plays a large part in the village economy.

One of the most traditional of all Yorkshire "shows" takes part in Muker in early September every year. Complete with Sheep Dog trials, dry stone walling demonstrations and livestock competitions.

For such a small village Muker has a surprising range of local services. There is the excellent **Farmers Arms** pub which does bar meals at lunch and in the evening. Next door is a **tea room / restaurant / local shop** affair **Muker Village Stores**, which also does **B&B**. Across the road is a set of well-maintained **public toilets** and **telephone box**. A large **car park** is situated 50-60 yards beyond the village by the bridge.

76 Walking the Herriot Way

Muker sits on the Service 30 **bus route** between Keld and Richmond, one stop along from Thwaite.

MUKER TO HERRIOT WAY PATH (HIGH ROUTE)

These notes will help you return to the traditional Herriot Way route, if you are planning on taking the high route to Reeth over the lead mines. Distance to rejoin the path at Keld: Approx 3 miles (5 km) -1½ to 2 hours

1. There are two paths leaving Muker to the north of the tiny village and we need the western path which runs along a tarmac lane, initially between two buildings then into a lane with a wall on the left and a hedge on the right. In comparison, the other path (the eastern one of the two) runs between two smaller buildings and then to a wide gate into the hay meadows.

2. Go along the lane, passing a building on the left and then out into open fields along what is now a farm track. The track climbs steeply and after ½ mile or so passes through a gate. Beyond this, walls begin to encroach on both sides and the gradient flattens out.

3. As the track turns left to pass through another gate, we keep straight ahead, across the grass to meet another wide gate that gives onto a narrow path between walls.

4. After a few yards we lose the wall on the right, but we keep straight ahead beside the wall on our left to meet a stone barn and a fingerpost. We are now back on the traditional Herriot Way path and you should continue reading from point 8 on page 72.

MUKER TO HERRIOT WAY PATH (LOW ROUTE)

These notes will help you return to the Herriot Way route, if you are planning on taking the low route to Reeth along the River Swale. Distance to rejoin the path at Ramps Holme Bridge: Approx ½ mile (1 km) - 15 to 20 mins

1. There are two paths leaving Muker to the north of the tiny village and we need the eastern one that runs to the right of **Stoneleigh B&B**, between a low building with a post box in front of it and the stone wall of a barn. The path quickly meets a wide gate that gives onto a hay meadow.

Section Two - Hawes to Keld

2. What is initially a wide track soon becomes a thin paved path through the meadows. It passes a couple of large field barns and cuts through half a dozen gated stiles before it reaches the bank of the River Swale.

3. Turn right at this final gate and follow the path beside the river to reach Ramps Holme Bridge. We are now back on the low level alternative Herriot Way route to Reeth and you should continue reading from point 1 on page 93.

SECTION THREE - KELD TO REETH (HIGH ROUTE)
Approx 11 miles (18 km)

Beyond Keld the path says goodbye to rolling green fells and fields and climbs into the bleak and blasted landscape of Gunnerside Moor, changed forever by the lead mining industry that ranged across the moors for decades. The heather however, remains a glorious site despite the industry and now supports the new "industry" of grouse shooting. The Way soon returns to the valley and the wonderful River Swale at Healaugh, before the short walk through fields into Reeth.

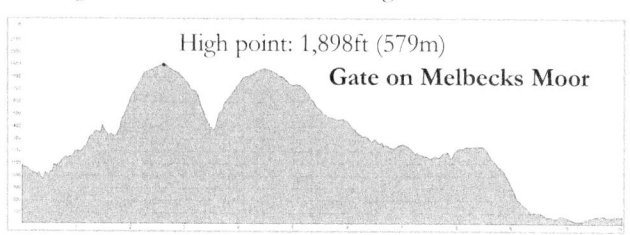

High point: 1,898ft (579m)

Gate on Melbecks Moor

Elevation Profile: Day 3 (High)

If you stayed in Muker last night, see page 77 for the notes needed to rejoin today's route.

PART 1 - KELD TO BLAKETHWAITE PEAT STORE
Approx 3½ miles (6 km) - 1½ to 2 hours

1. Leave Keld on the footpath at the bottom (north) end of the village. This path supports the Pennine Way, Wainwright's Coast to Coast path, the Swale Trail and the Herriot Way and takes us down a narrow lane between fields. Look back and say farewell to Keld; surely the busiest little village in Yorkshire.

2. 200 yards or so along the path and we come to a fork (NY 89503 01039). Keep to the left and drop steeply downhill on a well-made stone path, constructed in 2018 to support the newly opened Swale Trail. At the bottom we find a wide footbridge over the River Swale.

A short diversion to the right before we cross the bridge, through the gate and along the footpath beside the river, gives the best views of the lower of the two drops in East Gill Force.

3. Cross the bridge and turn left, following the path as it climbs up and over the upper drop of East Gill Force to a gate. If we hadn't only just started for the day this would be a fine spot for a break.

4. Go over the bridge, through the gate and follow the wide stony path as it climbs gently around the face of Beldi Hill. If it has rained recently you will probably be able to hear the water crashing through Kisdon Force below.

5. As the climb flattens out, pass through a gate and follow the path, straight now, for about ¼ of a mile to where it bends left and then right around an old field barn to the right of the path. Views open up to your right along this section showing the Swale as it sweeps down between high hills into Swaledale proper.

6. The path brings us to a rather incongruous old tractor parked on the path many years ago and left to rot. Keep to the path beside the broken wall and then within 40-50 yards bear left at another fork (NY 90482 00861). The track climbs gently for 200-300 yards until we arrive at Crackpot Hall.

There is evidence of a building here as far back as the 1500s, when a hunting lodge was maintained for Thomas the first Lord Wharton who liked to hunt the local red deer. The building that we see today though is the remains of the farmhouse that was built in the mid-18th century. It had a slate roof and "shippons" or cow sheds at each end for animals. The building was eventually abandoned in the 1950s due to subsidence.

7. The path skirts to the left of Crackpot Hall and then turns right (east), up the hill and beneath the face of a large spoil heap towards another building to the left of the path. This old stone barn would provide some shelter from the rain, as the roof is still mainly intact.

8. The stony path from the barn, with the jaw dropping view to the right soon becomes a green track through the bracken and brings us to a gate in a wall (NY 90977 00891); we are now turning up into Swinner Gill.

9. The path beyond the gate is narrow and rocky and stays high on the side of the hill above Swinner Gill with great views ahead and behind. It soon begins to descend though and within 400 yards it reaches an old packhorse bridge crossing a deep scar in the valley floor.

10. On the other side of the bridge is what remains of Swinner Gill Lead Mine. The path is visible ahead as it climbs beside the stream of East Grain and picks its way uncertainly through fallen stone and mining spoil.

11. About 200-250 yards after leaving the mine ruins the thin rocky path widens into a green space with a fingerpost pointing left up a flight of stone steps. These were added in 2018 and have vastly improved what was once a badly eroded and often wet and boggy path.

12. The path climbs steadily up the gill, on slabs for the most part, for a little over ¼ of a mile until it crosses a small slab bridge and a final flight of steps to a four-wheel drive track.

13. Turn left onto this new track, ignoring the footpath marked by the fingerpost on the other side and climb gently up towards the skyline. The road undulates as it climbs before flattening out and heading straight across the moor. Just under ½ a mile after joining the track we pass a large enclosure on our left that protects sheep from the dangers within and arrive at a gate in a fence line (NY 92550 01199).

14. A few yards after passing through the gate there is a double fingerpost which identifies that we are walking part of the "C. to C." or Coast to Coast path and another four-wheel drive track, which we ignore, branches off left and heads up the hill.

15. Continue along the road for perhaps 500-600 yards, until you see a large, ugly, corrugated iron sheepfold to the left, almost immediately beyond this you will see a pair of small

cairns, also on the left of the road, marking a narrow path that heads off left through the heather (NY 93188 01309).

16. Leave the track here and follow this path. The path cuts through the heather, skirting close to North Hush, with cairns to guide us. Over the next ½ a mile the path widens and the cairns become less frequent. The path is quite badly eroded in places and has one or two steep sections as it drops down and leaves the heather behind.

17. More mine ruins come into view at the bottom of the valley. Before we get there though, the path crosses a dried up stream using a natural stone shelf and then turns sharp right, almost back on itself and then sharp left to join a wider path leading down to the river and the ruins of Blakethwaite Peat Store.

The smelt mill at a lead mine burned coal (if they could get it) and peat for the most part. This would be cut from the surrounding hills and stored in long, open-fronted buildings called peat stores, to dry out. The one at Blakethwaite was about 80-100 feet long and most of the arches remain intact. The one above Old Gang Mill, further along today's walk was over 100 yards in length and had 40 arches.

While descending to Blakethwaite Peat Store, look out for the path on the opposite hillside that climbs from behind the peat store and zig zags upwards to another path about half way up the side of the hill. This is the path we will be using to exit the valley in a few minutes.

---

18. There is plenty to explore here, including a fine stone slab bridge across the gill, an old lime kiln and other supporting buildings.

PART 2 - BLAKETHWAITE PEAT STORE TO SURRENDER BRIDGE
Approx 4 miles (6 km) - 2 to 2½ hours

1. When you are ready to leave, find the narrow path behind the main building (the long peat store with the arches) and follow it steeply right, then left, then right again until it meets a wide green path and a cairn.

2. Turn right onto this path and follow it for a short distance as it runs between the bracken and below a slope covered in limestone scree. No more than 100 yards after we joined it, our path meets the edge of the scree and you will find a break in the bracken border and see a thin green path turning sharp left and heading across the scree slope (NY 93842 01652). Take this path.

3. The thin path is stony for the first couple of hundred yards, but then becomes a narrow grassy path, turning gently right as it climbs the hill. The path continues to turn steadily right, essentially describing a large inverted U as it climbs up. The occasional cairn guides the way, but the path is easy to follow, albeit a bit wet after rain.

4. The last couple of hundred yards of the path cut through the heather and we reach a pair of cairns beside a four-wheel drive track that supports the shooting hut at Blakethwaite Lead Mines.

5. Turn right (south) onto the four-wheel drive track and follow it as it cuts through the heather. After about 100 yards we will pass a fingerpost marked "FP Keld".

6. The heather now struggles to find any foothold among the wasteland of tips and spoil heaps and soon peters out almost completely, leaving us to walk through a barren moonscape of stone and gravel.

You are now passing through Old Gang Mine, the source of the ore that was processed further down the valley in the Smelting Mills you will see soon.

---

7. The path is not so distinct now and care should be taken in poor conditions; keep to the track defined by vehicle wheels, shunning any diversions to the left or right. Approximately mid-way across the plateau an old, rust-coloured piece of mine machinery can be found beside the path to the left (NY 94885 01424). The only landmark in a sea of rocks and stones.

8. Approximately 300 yards after passing the old stone breaker we will come to a pair of grouse butts, standing sentinel on either side of the path. These are part of a

much longer chain of butts running across Melbecks Moor.

9. From here, the road now winds and descends between spoil heaps with a barren expanse of heather moorland to the left. Follow the road and within ½ a mile of passing the grouse butts we will pass a large cairn on the left of the path and a huge spoil heap on the right (NY 95753 01428).

10. The landscape begins to soften, as the heather returns and the spoil heaps become less prevalent. The road descends gently with a ditch to the right and a broken stone wall beyond. Within ½ a mile of the cairn the road reaches Level House Bridge.

11. Cross the bridge and go through the kissing gate, following the road as it continues to descend, winding between gravel tips with a heather-clad bank on the left. After about 400 yards there is a gentle left turn, the road heads uphill slightly and 100 yards further on the road branches. Keep to the main track here, to the right.

12. A further 200 yards along the road and you will see another road heading off to the right, across a narrow bridge and up to the moorland where it provides access to a number of grouse shooting sites. This is another diversion you should ignore.

13. Continue along the track and within a couple of minutes the buildings at Old Gang come into view.

On the hillside to the left are a series of broken pillars, standing in a long row. These are the remains of the immense peat store. Peat was cut from the surrounding moors and stored and dried before feeding the fires of the Smelt Mill. Each mill had its own peat store. These buildings are easy to identify by their open fronts, which allowed the peat to dry quicker. Further down the track you will see a couple of smaller buildings and the chimney of the mill.

---

14. The first of the small buildings is now a shooting hut, locked tight against unwanted visitors, but the outhouse at the back, with a portable toilet, may be unlocked. This hut and its larger brother a little way ahead, are both converted

mine buildings, but now support the shooting sites on the moorland opposite. A fine old packhorse bridge crosses the beck on the other side of the road from the hut.

A packhorse bridge is a bridge designed to carry packhorses over a river. Traditionally the bridge is wide enough for one horse only and has low, or no, parapets so as not to interfere with the loaded panniers carried by the horses. You will see several such bridges along the route.

15. The second hut, just a few yards further along, will also almost certainly be locked tight. The hut is lined with benches, so in good weather this is also a good rest stop.

16. Another 100 yards and the remains of the Old Gang Smelting Mill will come into view; the tall chimney acting as a stark landmark among the broken ruins and spoil heaps (NY 97435 00527). History abounds here and most visitors will find it hard to pass by without exploring.

17. Leave Old Gang Smelting Mill behind and climb gently along the road, which now hugs Mill Gill quite closely, before climbing slightly above it, cutting through dense heather, richly populated with grouse which will explode from cover and fly off with a loud, startling cackle as we approach. Almost exactly one mile from the mill, the four-wheel drive track arrives at Surrender Bridge which carries the moorland road connecting Swaledale and Arkengarthdale over Mill Gill.

This road was made famous by the opening credits of the All Creatures Great & Small TV series. Less than a mile up the road is the ford through which James and Siegfried splash in their car.

PART 3 - SURRENDER BRIDGE TO REETH
Approx 3½ miles (6 km) - 1½ to 2 hours

1. The path continues straight ahead (west), across the road, directed by a fingerpost on the opposite side. The path splits soon after we join it, and the right hand track is the one that brings us the closer to Surrender Smelt Mill. This is a fascinating ruin and has decayed in such a way that the

individual parts of the smelting process can be seen. There is an information board inside the building with more details.

The flue for the Smelting Mill runs several hundred yards underground to a chimney on the hillside to the north west - as you leave the mill behind, look back and you can still see its broken remains. The flue is exposed in one or two places and you can see how small and narrow it is. Boys were used to clean the flue and to recover re-usable material from it.

---

2. There is a clear and obvious path leading east, away from the mill, but this isn't the one we should be using. Instead find a small green track that runs north from the rear of the mill, uphill, into the heather. We're heading for the cairn that's visible on the hill just a short way north and east of the mill.

3. The green track turns east almost immediately after leaving the area of the ruins of the mill, but if in doubt head for the cairn. The path runs through the heather and can be boggy in places after rain.

4. From the cairn (NY 99363 00016) the path runs along the upper slope of Bleaberry Gill, before reaching the edge of the small valley. From here we can look east and see our path as it follows the wall on the other side of the gill. There are steps to help us descend the steep bank and a wooden footbridge to cross the beck.

5. The climb out of the little valley is possibly the steepest climb anywhere on the Herriot Way, but fortunately is only a few dozen feet of ascent before we reach a wooden gate in the wall at the top.

6. Beyond the gate the path runs beside the wall to our right and we may encounter one or two boggy sections along here after rains. After 200-300 yards the wall runs out, but the path continues in the same direction, picking up a four-wheel drive track that cuts through the heather.

7. After about 200-300 yards more, this track splits; the more obvious track continuing straight on, but we need to bear right here (SE 00455 99954). Head downhill towards the

wall of a large sheepfold, which we keep to our left, heading for the large house (Nova Scotia); with surely one of the best views you could ask for.

8. Path selection at the house is crucial. The obvious four-wheel drive track heading due east away from the house should be shunned in favour of an unclear path that runs downhill between the wall of the house on our right and the wall of a field on the left. Although unclear at first this path soon becomes a green track between the rougher moorland grasses and bracken.

9. The path sticks close to the wall on our right and after 300 yards or so describes a long S; turning steeply down right and then left before arriving at a stile in the wall (or a large gate; as the stile is easy to miss if the bracken is fully grown). Use either method to enter the field.

10. The field contains a sunken basin with a tap, which is as good a guide as any to an old iron gate (SE 01014 99281), beneath tall pines, leading into the wood beyond.

11. Once through the gate, turn left and follow the path through the wood for a hundred yards or so climbing up to an open space beneath the trees with a low wire fence and a tall hedge facing us.

12. Bear right here (left takes us into the drive of Thiernswood Hall); leaving the wood and walking down a long drive between low fences, which soon becomes tree-lined. Follow this lane for ¼ of a mile or so until we approach a stone barn on the left of the lane. About 10-20 yards beyond this barn, in the wall on the left of the lane, is a narrow gated stile leading into a field (SE 01383 99024).

13. Follow the path through this field, using either the gate or the narrow stile to enter the field beyond, to our right. We cut the corner of this field heading for another narrow stile in the wall ahead.

14. This stile gives on to a large field and we follow the wall on our left until it brings us to another small stile beside large trees. Go through the stile and turn right into a narrow unkempt track between two walls which, after a hundred yards or so bends right and then left and becomes

a tarmac lane which leads down into the tiny village of Healaugh, beside the telephone box.

HEALAUGH
📞

This small village is pronounced "Hee Law" but unfortunately hardly deserves the title "village". There is nothing to interest a weary walker here; no tea room, no pub, just a couple of benches and a telephone box.

The lonely **telephone box** is situated in a small, three sided courtyard beside the main road running through the village.

15. Turn left (east) along the road through the village. As we pass the last house on the right (The Manor House), look for a stile in the wall beside a barn next to the road a little way ahead. Ignore the much more obvious footpath heading downhill beside a prominent fingerpost.

16. The stile beside the barn has a much less obvious fingerpost pointing us to "FP Reeth" (SE 01971 99061). The path runs through a number of fields, staying some height above the River Swale and offering increasingly lovely views to the right as we progress towards Reeth.

17. For the next mile (as far as the outskirts of Reeth) the path is easy to follow as it runs between field boundaries. You can use the list that follows to tick off the gates and stiles as you pass through them:

    Narrow stile beside "FP Reeth" fingerpost, narrow gated stile, narrow stile beside barn, narrow stile with steps, narrow stile, open gateway beneath tree, narrow stile, narrow gated stile almost immediately followed by narrow stile, narrow stile, narrow gated stile, narrow gated stile beside wide wooden gate.

18. From this gate you can look right, down to the River Swale and Reeth's 'swing' bridge across to the far bank. Ahead of us we bear left, not climbing the bank but using a sunken path between the bank and a wall on our right.

19. This leads us to a final narrow gate (SE 03455 99125), beside a much larger metal vehicle gate which gives onto

a narrow lane between stone walls. This soon becomes a tarmac lane; passing a children's playground and a medical centre on the left.

20. About 250-300 yards after passing through the last gate we will meet a residential road coming from the left to join our little lane. Follow the fingerpost here that points us left, towards Reeth, along the residential road.

21. After a hundred yards or so take the first right into a smaller lane beside a row of houses, which then turns left into an even narrower lane. A further hundred yards along, this lane turns right into what looks like a courtyard, surrounded by houses. Follow this to the end and we enter the centre of Reeth village - right between two pubs.

REETH

Reeth is another town that can be dated as far back as the Domesday book. In there it was called "Rie" which is the ancient Anglo-Saxon name for a ditch, beck or river.

The most prominent feature of Reeth is its village green, a large, gently sloping expanse of well-maintained grass surrounded by picturesque shops, pubs and houses. Reeth is a great place to stock up on supplies, send a few postcards and sample some fabulous Black Sheep ale.

Reeth has ample accommodation options including **several B&Bs** and three **pub-type hotels** as well as a **hotel / restaurant** at the top of the village green. More detailed accommodation information can be obtained from the National Park Centre located in the village.

The village has three pubs, all located around the green; the **Black Bull**, the **Kings Arms** and the **Buck Hotel**; all are popular with walkers and offer food as well as traditional pub fare.

There is ample **parking** in Reeth around the central village green. A **telephone box** is located at the top of the village green (top meaning both north and most elevated end) beside the **bus stop** and **public toilets**. There are several **tea rooms** and even an **ice-cream parlour**. As with most of the facilities in the village the majority are located around the village green.

The **bus stop** at the top end of the village beside the Buck Hotel, is serviced by the following bus routes; 30, 36 and 480R running between Richmond and Keld. There are three **general stores** in Reeth, one of which also includes the **Post Office**, situated on the east side of the green. As well as the tea rooms and the pubs which all serve food there is also a **restaurant** at the very top of the village in the **Burgoyne Hotel**. The **Copper Kettle** tea room has an extensive menu including main meals. Although there is no pharmacy in the village, the Post Office has basic first aid supplies and common "over the counter" **medicines**.

SECTION THREE - KELD TO REETH (LOW ROUTE)
Approx 12 miles (19 km)

From leaving Keld to arriving in Reeth we are never far from the banks of the River Swale and often we are walking hand-in-hand with this iconic river. We drop down through Kisdon Gorge at the head of Swaledale and use paths through the hay meadows to reach Gunnerside. Beyond we cross the Swale and follow riverside paths until we cross again, on Reeth's wonderful footbridge before arriving in the village itself.

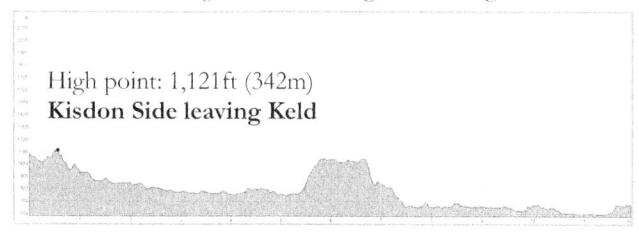

High point: 1,121ft (342m)
Kisdon Side leaving Keld

Elevation Profile: Day 3 (Low)

If you stayed in Muker last night, see page 77 for the notes needed to rejoin today's route.

PART 1 - KELD TO RAMPS HOLME BRIDGE
Approx 2½ miles (4 km) - 1 to 1½ hours

1. Leave Keld on the footpath at the bottom (north) end of the village. This path supports the Pennine Way, Wainwright's Coast to Coast path, the Swale Trail and the Herriot Way and takes us down a narrow lane between fields. Look back and say farewell to Keld; surely the busiest little village in Yorkshire.

2. 200 yards or so along the path and we come to a fork (NY 89503 01039). Keep straight ahead, on the upper path signposted to Thwaite/Muker. A rugged track soon brings us to a wide wooden gate, beyond which the track drops gently with an embankment on the right.

3. Keep an eye open on the right for a fingerpost which points down to Kisdon Force. This impressive waterfall

requires a diversion (steeply downhill) of no more than ¼ of a mile all told and if you have time is well worth it.

4. Our lovely rugged track climbs gently now, beneath a huge rock wall on the right and after 100-150 yards or so meets another fingerpost beside two large earth mounds (NY 89804 00857). We keep left here and the track descends again, now sunken between banks and with views of Kisdon Gorge beginning to open up.

5. Across the valley on our left, almost at the same level, is the path of the high route to Reeth and the remains of Crackpot Hall (see page 80). The track is easy to follow, twisting and turning beneath trees and soon arrives at another wooden gate. Beyond, the path becomes easier on the feet, now mostly grass covered and lined by broken stones on each side. Aim for the barn visible ahead.

6. We don't actually reach the barn, the path descends gently left away from it, now lined only on our left, heading for another barn instead. When we reach it we find a fingerpost at its corner, pointing us towards Muker (NY 90485 00527).

7. The path is still obvious, across grass now, with occasional stones to help us across one or two boggy patches. After a couple of hundred yards we pass another barn (on our right) and a view of the Swale opens up before us. To our left is the great gap of Swinner Gill and Kisdon looms large on our right.

8. Follow the track down into the valley, crossing a broken wall and shortly after joining a dry stone wall beside a large tree. Follow the wall on our left, crossing another broken wall (NY 90789 00177) and passing two barns, one on our left and one on our right. We are now in the bottom of the valley with steep hills on all sides.

9. We cross two more broken walls and then use a gap stile in an intact dry stone wall, the track still well-worn and obvious ahead. After crossing another broken wall we reach the bank of the Swale. It would be hard to get lost now with the river as a hand-rail on our left.

10. 200 yards or so after meeting the river, the path passes beneath some trees and through a wooden gate. Climb the bank beyond and follow the now somewhat muddy track to a metal gate. The next ½ mile sees us pass through two ungated walls, pass a barn on our right and narrow gated stile in a wall. The path now runs along the top of a grassy bank with another barn visible ahead.

11. As we approach the barn we find a stunted fingerpost (SD 90813 98771) pointing back to Keld, but we keep head, passing the barn on our right and following the broken wall on the left. After 100 yards or so we bend left, pass through a narrow gated stile and follow a thin path beside the river. We pass the turn off to Muker on our right and continue through another narrow gate to reach Ramps Holme Bridge (SD 91021 98595), over the river Swale.

PART 2 - RAMPS HOLME BRIDGE TO ISLES BRIDGE
Approx 5 miles (8 km) - 2½ to 3 hours

1. Cross the bridge and turn right at the far side, climbing the stone steps and following the fingerpost to Gunnerside. The path is rocky and uneven beneath the trees, and the river bends away from us.

2. The going becomes flatter and easier as we approach Ramps Holme Farm. Pass through a narrow gated stile and pick your own path through the field beyond, aiming just to the right of the buildings ahead.

3. At the farm we find another gated stile in a dry stone wall (SD 91188 98296) and a mostly clear path across the next field to a narrow stile beside a wide metal gate beneath trees.

4. Bear half left through the next field, aiming for the wide gap in the wall ahead, to the right of a field barn. As you get closer you will see a gated stile in the wall, beside a fingerpost. Continue straight ahead through the next field to another gated stile.

5. Continue straight ahead again, through the next long field before eventually arriving at another gated stile, fingerpost and the River Swale. Beyond the stile, we stick close to the

Swale, hemmed in between fences for 100 yards or so until we are forced to cross a stile beside a wide wooden gate.

6. Turn right onto a four wheel drive track that climbs gently up and soon opens into a wide pasture. Look out for the fingerpost on our right (SD 91757 97925), following the finger to "Ivelet Bridge" and dropping down the bank to walk beside the river.

7. After 100 yards pass through a narrow gated stile to enter a long meadow with a bank on the left. Keep to the right, beside the river, following the obvious green track. After 500-600 yards the path bends left and becomes a thin rocky track climbing into the trees, beneath a wooded slope.

8. Keep to this sometime tricky path with its exposed tree roots and low hanging branches until we reach a wooden gate and emerge into long narrow pasture. Close cropped grass replaces the tricky tree roots and we pass a field barn on our left as we progress beside the river.

9. About 350 yards after entering the pasture, we use a narrow gated stile beside a metal gate and continue ahead, now with the grassy bank close on our left. We are soon forced to climb this bank and at its top the path bends left, up towards a narrow wooden gate at the far left end of the wall in front of us (SD 92875 97763).

10. The pasture beyond is wide and you are free to choose your own path across it, heading towards the river on the right. Pass through a wide gap in a wall and a few dozen yards beyond this we reach the graceful span of Ivelet Bridge.

In this area, packhorses were the main form of goods transport until the 1880s. Fords were the usual ways of crossing rivers, but Ivelet is fortunate to have one of the finest packhorse bridges in the Dales. Dating from 1695, it is also reputed to be haunted by a headless dog.

Ivelet Bridge (also known as Satron Bridge) was part of the Swaledale Corpse Road (the route taken to bring the dead to consecrated ground) and a coffin stone sits here, at the end of the riverside parapet. Mourners would rest here, standing the coffin on the stone, while they caught their breath.

11. Go through the gate set in the bridge parapet and continue straight ahead, along the tarmac lane. The lane climbs gently to begin, then more steeply as it bends left into the village of Ivelet. At the top of the climb, turn right in front of the red telephone box.

12. After a couple of dozen yards the lane enters a farm yard and we take a footpath on the right, marked by a fingerpost, dropping down into the trees. At the bottom of the slope, cross a narrow wooden footbridge (SD 93707 98012) and climb steeply up the other side, through a narrow gated stile and into a hay meadow.

13. Aim slightly left into the field; there should be an obvious path to follow at most times of the year, this being a popular footpath. We soon reach a narrow gated stile, a little to the left of a wide metal gate, in the dry stone wall.

14. Cross the next meadow to reach another gated stile and cross the next meadow, aiming for the field barn. Before we reach it go through another narrow gated stile and then follow the path to the left of the barn. Beyond, the path goes around a large tree and through another gated stile in a wall.

15. Climb the little bank and cross another wide meadow, the River Swale visible down the slope on our right. Go through another gated stile and keeping to the already worn path through the meadow, bend gently left, up towards a field barn.

16. At the barn we find a choice of gaps in the wall that take us into the next field. Keep to the right and aim for the right hand end of the wall ahead, where we find another gated stile. On the other side we find ourselves walking along the top of a steep bank, with the river at its bottom.

17. Another gated stile soon takes us into a wide sloping meadow. The view into Swaledale from here is majestic and never more so than in the summer when the flowers

paint the fields in glorious colour. The roofs of the houses of Gunnerside are now visible too.

18. Keep to the fence on the right to begin, but we soon bend left away from it, and cross the meadow to reach another gated stile in a wall. Keep ahead across the next field, and through a wide gate and across the next to a narrow gap stile.

19. Only two more fields now! Cross the next meadow to reach a gated stile beside tall trees and then bear half left through the next field, aiming for the houses. Here we find a narrow wooden gate set in a stone wall beside a house (SD 94942 98138).

20. Go through the gate and skirt around the house on our left, following the paved path up to a gate beside a bench and a yellow grit container. This brings us to a tarmac lane, onto which we turn left, passing some houses and out into the village. We emerge at the tiniest village green anywhere in the Dales, but it has plenty of seating.

GUNNERSIDE

In Old Norse, Gunnerside was "Gunnar's Saetr", so we must presume that it was a Norseman called Gunnar who first established the settlement, probably around the 10th century. In the 19th century it was a major site for the lead mining industry and the village provides relatively easy access to some of the best-preserved remains of the Swaledale mining industry.

At the heart of the village is the **Kings Head** pub, which is open from noon every day and serves food at lunch time between noon and 2pm and in the evening between 6pm and 8.45pm. On the other side of the road are **two tea rooms**, the **Ghyllfoot** and **Mary Shaws Café**. The village has a small number of **parking** places, and a set of **public toilets** just down the path beside the pub. A small working **Smithy** is located in the village alongside an excellent **museum** showing local history.

96   Walking the Herriot Way

Gunnerside is serviced by **bus route 30**; between Keld and Richmond. This service runs twice a day, Monday to Saturday to Keld, but more often to Richmond. At weekends and Bank Holidays, this is replaced by the **less frequent 830** service. Services and schedules are seasonal, so check availability before relying on a service.

Gunnerside is thought to have given its name to the most successful act of sabotage in all of World War II, as the commandos who carried out the raid trained nearby. In February 1943, Operation Gunnerside succeeded in destroying the German heavy water production facilities in Norway, being used as part of their attempts to develop nuclear weapons.

21. Go over the bridge, past the pub and tea rooms and up the road leading out of the village. At the last house on the right bear left onto a steep tarmac lane, barred by a wide metal gate, but with a narrow wooden gate beside it for walkers. Climb up the lane.

22. As the lane turns sharply left, we bear right onto a rough track that climbs steeply beneath the trees. The track soon emerges, still climbing onto the open hillside, with incredible views back down Swaledale. A few yards more and we meet a wall on the left and then cross a narrow beck beneath trees.

23. Coming out of the trees we pass a large barn and continue ascending, now between tall walls. A little further on and we pass the remains of two cottages at Lane Foot. A little way beyond and the path widens, but we keep closer to the wall on our right.

24. As the houses at Heights come into view, look for a stone step stile in the wall on our right (SD 95964 98188). It's easy to miss and if you arrive at a wooden gate in the wall you may need to backtrack a few yards. The view from the top of the stile was worth the climb!

25. In the next field we are aiming for a gap stile about central in the length of the wall, not the wide gap at its top. Beyond, aim for another gap stile in line with the power

pole and in the next field, cross under the power lines and aim for a stone step stile to the right of the tall trees.

26. The next field crossing is short and the small white sign for Rowleth Woods is visible beside the gap stile that leads into this charming managed woodland.

27. The woods themselves may be charming and a welcome distraction from the fields we have been crossing so far, but the path through them is worthy of special care. It can be very slippery after rain and as much as you'll be wanting to admire the scenery, one eye at least should be on your feet at all times.

28. It's just short of ½ a mile between the two stone walls that encompass Rowleth Woods. As we emerge from the far one (SD 96847 97748) we are deposited onto a sloping pasture, home to hundreds of rabbits.

29. Follow the contour of the hill to meet a wide gap in a stone wall, followed by a slightly narrower gap in the next wall and an even thinner gap in the one beyond. The grassy path now climbs gently for 100 yards or so to meet a wide wooden gate with the buildings of Smarber further up the hillside.

30. Go through the gate and bear half right, downhill passing close to the power pole and aiming for the wide metal gate beyond it. In the next field make your own way to the wide wooden gate directly below us, beside the field barn (SD 97303 97571).

31. A very short diversion, right, along the front of the field barn, brings us to a walled enclosure. This is all that remains of Smarber Chapel. A stone plaque on the wall is all that identifies it.

The Toleration Act of 1689 allowed freedom of worship and many Dales folk chose to follow the Congregationalists and Presbyterians. Smarber Chapel, above Low Row was the first non-conformist chapel in Swaledale, built in 1690 by Phillip Lord Wharton, who owned local land and lead mines. It was replaced in 1809 by the Congregational Chapel in Low Row.

32. Retrace your steps back to the gate and continue ahead (left if you've just come out of the gate) following the wall on our left. We soon meet another wooden gate with a picturesque beck tumbling down from the hillside just beyond it.

33. Follow the faint green path straight ahead across the meadow, passing a lone tree and a fenced off enclosure, eventually arriving at a wide wooden gate in a wall. Go through and continue for about 50-60 yards, keeping an eye out for a wooden post with a yellow way marker on it. Just before you reach this, look for a path that cuts back, down into the trees on our right (SD 97766 97732).

34. At the bottom of the path go through the wide gate and turn immediately left, down a set of steps to reach a road. Turn left along the road for just a few yards, then cut right down beside a wall to meet another tarmac lane. Turn right onto this.

35. The lane drops down and crosses the River Swale on Isles Bridge.

Isles Bridge was first built in 1734, out of wood, but was washed away twice during floods. In 1801 a local farmer, Richard Garth, raised money to build a stone bridge. This too was badly damaged by flood in 1883 and had to be rebuilt.

PART 3 - ISLES BRIDGE TO REETH
Approx 4½ miles (7 km) - 2½ to 3 hours

1. On the far side of the bridge, turn left along the lane signposted "Low Houses only ¼" passing one of the best hidden telephone boxes in Yorkshire.

2. Follow the lane for 500-600 yards, where we come upon Lawn House, built in 1766 when the lead mining industry was producing incredible profits for the mine owners (SD 98213 97305). A few yards beyond this and we need to bear left, before entering a farm yard, along a track signposted "The Swale Trail and Low Whita".

3. Low Lane runs for 1½ miles between dry stone walls with intermittent views to the northern slopes of Swaledale and the houses and field barns dotted all over it. The lane

eventually brings us to the buildings at Low Whita (SE 00342 98202). There is a bunkhouse here. Turn left at the junction.

4. About ¼ of a mile from Low Whita we ignore a junction on the left leading to Scabba Wath bridge over the Swale.

Scabba Wath is thought to be the name given to a foot ford used by Roman soldiers travelling from their fort in Bainbridge to their more permanent camp at Greta Bridge.

5. We stay on the tarmac lane for another ¼ of a mile as it climbs gently and soon opens up with gorse and bracken on the right and the open fellside of Harkerside Moor beyond, a view towards tomorrow's path back to Aysgarth.

6. The road drops gently and then ascends gently again, passing a field barn on the left and soon reaching a set of power lines above our heads. As we pass beneath them, look for a fingerpost beside the wall on our left, pointing us along a narrow path between the wall and the gorse.

7. After 50-60 yards look for a gated stile set high in the wall (SE 01457 98362) and use this to enter a wide sloping pasture bounded by trees on the left and the wall on the right. At the far end of the pasture go through the sturdy wooden gate and continue beside the wall.

8. A steep slope drops away on our left now, down to the Swale flowing between trees and with great views across Swaledale to Calver Hill. After 400-500 yards the path begins to descend, still beside the wall to meet the river. Here we find another sturdy wooden gate and the weather-proof gravel track that supports the Swale Trail.

9. Look out for the stepping stones across the Swale (if the river hasn't risen to hide them) (SE 02082 98741) that would give access to Healaugh if there were any facilities there worth reaching (which there are not).

10. The gravel track is hard work on the feet in places, designed more for wheels (bikes, buggies and wheelchairs) than boots, but it hugs the river and offers plenty of places to sit and enjoy the water.

11. We pass through another gate and shortly after the gravel gives out and we are walking on springy turf again. Joy! A tree has fallen across the path just beyond a marker post (SE 02694 98891) and we must bend right, around it before picking up the river side path again.
12. Keep the river on your left for another ½ mile crossing a step stile in a wooden gate across our path before arriving at Reeth's iconic footbridge. Despite its name, the bridge is not designed to swing, but it's still a wonderful structure.

The bridge we see today was built in 2002 after the previous span, which had survived for 80 years and innumerable floods, was destroyed by an uprooted tree being washed down the swollen river in September 2000.

A local tale says the name of the bridge originates from the swinging motion the old bridge exhibited when enough kids crossed it and 'encouraged' it.

---

13. Bounce your way across the river and turn right at the far side, soon passing through a wooden gate into an area of newly planted trees. Follow the track until it reaches the river in front of us (SE 03456 98995), then turn left, across the wooden duck boards and up a wide track between walls to a wooden gate beside a barn.
14. Go through the gate and the path is now much narrower and over-arched by trees, climbing steeply to meet another track at the top. Turn right along this track, which soon becomes a tarmac lane; passing a children's playground and a medical centre on the left.
15. After about 250-300 yards we meet a residential road coming from the left to join our little lane. Follow the fingerpost here that points us left, towards the village.
16. After a hundred yards or so take the first right into a smaller lane beside a row of houses, which then turns left into an even narrower lane. A further hundred yards along, this lane turns right into what looks like a courtyard, surrounded by houses. Follow this to the end and we enter the centre of Reeth village, right between two pubs.

REETH

Reeth is another town that can be dated as far back as the Domesday book. In there it was called "Rie" which is the ancient Anglo-Saxon name for a ditch, beck or river.

The most prominent feature of Reeth is its village green, a large, gently sloping expanse of well-maintained grass surrounded by picturesque shops, pubs and houses. Reeth is a great place to stock up on supplies, send a few postcards and sample some fabulous Black Sheep ale.

Reeth has ample accommodation options including **several B&Bs** and three **pub-type hotels** as well as a **hotel / restaurant** at the top of the village green. More detailed accommodation information can be obtained from the National Park Centre located in the village.

The village has three pubs, all located around the green; the **Black Bull**, the **Kings Arms** and the **Buck Hotel**; all are popular with walkers and offer food as well as traditional pub fare.

There is ample **parking** in Reeth around the central village green. A **telephone box** is located at the top of the village green (top meaning both north and most elevated end) beside the **bus stop** and **public toilets**. There are several **tea rooms** and even an **ice-cream parlour**. As with most of the facilities in the village the majority are located around the village green.

The **bus stop** at the top end of the village beside the Buck Hotel, is serviced by the following bus routes; 30, 36 and 480R running between Richmond and Keld. There are three **general stores** in Reeth, one of which also includes the **Post Office**, situated on the east side of the green. As well as the tea rooms and the pubs which all serve food there is also a **restaurant** at the very top of the village in the **Burgoyne Hotel**. The **Copper Kettle** tea room has an extensive menu including main meals. Although there is no pharmacy in the village, the Post Office has basic first aid supplies and common "over the counter" **medicines**.

SECTION FOUR - REETH TO AYSGARTH
Approx 14 miles (23 km)

Leaving Reeth, the route heads south, climbing up to Grinton Lodge Hostel, right on the edge of the moors. A short hop from the hostel takes the path into the glorious heather and open moorland around Gibbon Hill and then along the rough but easy track through Apedale. After Dent's Houses the path drops steeply down to the village of Castle Bolton and the atmospheric remains of its castle. More fields and back lanes lead to the very impressive falls at Aysgarth and then back to the village itself.

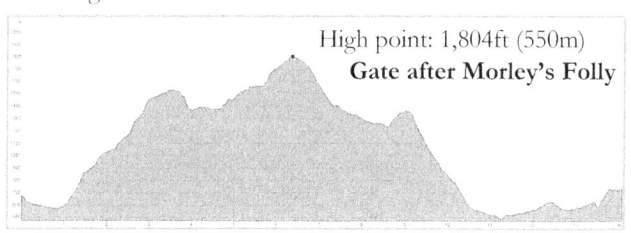

High point: 1,804ft (550m)
Gate after Morley's Folly

Elevation Profile: Day 4

PART 1 - REETH TO GRINTON LODGE
Approx 1½ miles (2 km) - 45 mins to 1 hour

1. We leave Reeth by the road to the south, downhill from the green and over the old road bridge over Arkle Beck.

2. Use the footpath beside the busy main road once we've crossed the bridge and after about 100-150 yards we come to a small kissing gate in the wall beside the road (SE 04266 99086) and a fingerpost points us along the narrow, sometimes muddy riverside path.

3. The path is shaded by trees but these are soon left behind as we pass through a narrow gate into a large field. The path across the field is contained by two fences, so route finding is effortless, if somewhat constricted.

4. The gravel path between the fences, passes through a pair of gates, before heading for the three-span bridge that takes the main road over the River Swale and into Grinton.

The bridge has stone steps set into it, leading up to a narrow gate.

5. Turn right through the gate and follow the pavement into Grinton village.

GRINTON (INC. GRINTON LODGE HOSTEL)

There are only a handful of buildings in Grinton and this has always been the case, so it seems unusual that such a small village should have such an imposing church as St. Andrews. It was originally built in the time of the Normans but has been added to over the intervening centuries. It is one of the most important medieval buildings in the whole of Swaledale though and is Grade I listed. One of the grave stones in the churchyard is Grade II listed - that of Richard Clarkson - have a look, see if you can find it.

The other building of importance in the village is of course the pub, the Bridge Inn. This offers the only amenities in the village and is within an easy stagger of the Youth Hostel. Just remember to take a torch with you for the return journey, as there are no street lights on the road up the hill!

The only accommodation in Grinton itself is at the **Bridge Inn**. About ½ a mile up the road though is the Youth Hostel at **Grinton Lodge**, an old hunting lodge with plenty of space and large airy common rooms.

A **telephone box** is located behind the Bridge Inn, a short distance along the B6270, beside the old Grinton Literary Institute building.

Grinton's small **public convenience** building is situated just beside the telephone box.

There is a **bus stop**, located on the road behind the pub, next to the telephone box. Grinton is serviced by routes 30, 36 and 480R running between Richmond and Keld.

The **Bridge Inn** serves food; both bar food and in a separate, fine dining restaurant section.

Almost the first building we come to is the Bridge Inn, which has the strangest roof ornament of any building on the Herriot Way. A sheep, often decorated to celebrate local events, can be seen keeping watch over the village from the roof of the pub. A tuba, a guitar and a bicycle wheel have all been recent additions to the Swaledale on the roof.

6. The Youth Hostel is ½ a mile up the road, but this is a narrow and quite busy lane so resist the temptation and instead turn left (east) beside the pub and follow the main road with its wide pavement for about 150 yards. As the road starts to bend left look for a fingerpost and a pair of narrow gated stiles in the wall on the other side of the road (SE 04837 98301). Take the left hand one of the two stiles and enter the field, with the wall to our right.

7. Follow the path as it climbs the hill beside the wall on our right. The crenulated tower of Grinton Lodge can be seen ahead on the skyline. The path passes through a wide, open gateway in a wall and heads for the field barn in the wall on the other side of the field.

8. Go through the narrow gate to the left of the barn and head across the field to another narrow gated stile set high in the wall, with steps set into the wall. Beyond this the path goes through a wide, open gateway in a wall and then up to a gate between two large buildings.

9. Go through the gate and head uphill to meet the road which takes us the 200 yards or so up to the Grinton Lodge Youth Hostel.

SHORT-CUT: GRINTON LODGE TO DENT'S HOUSES
Approx 3 miles (5 km) - 1½ to 2 hours

Please consider that this short-cut may not be the best route to follow in poor weather, especially in poor visibility. The usual route, round Gibbon Hill, although longer, is easier to follow in mist or low cloud and offers more possibility of shelter from strong wind and rain, than does this short-cut over Greets Hill.

(If taking the short-cut, this description replaces all of Part 2 and points 1 to 5 in Part 3 below)

1. With Grinton Lodge at your back, cross the road and follow the bridleway, indicated by the fingerpost, through the heather to another fingerpost.

2. At the tarmac road, turn left and follow the road as it climbs steeply up the hill. As the road bends to the left, stay on the road, ignoring the bridleway to the right, which would take us on the traditional route to Aysgarth.

3. The climb soon reaches a crest and flattens out somewhat, the road visible ahead into the distance. Ignore early diversions to the right; a four-wheel drive track and then a narrow green track through the heather.

4. Once the climb flattens perceptibly you will see a fingerpost with several information boards attached to it, pointing out a bridleway across the moorland (SE 03843 96330). Leave the road here, stepping over a small stream and follow an indistinct green path across the moor.

5. In clear weather our destination is easily visible; a pair of large cairns ahead on the crest of the hill. In poor visibility you will need to keep an eye to the ground to follow the green path closely.

6. The path is generally straight, but meanders here and there to avoid patches of heather and stony areas. It soon passes between a raised heather embankment and the occasional cairn.

7. Our path soon meets another, which supports the grouse butts in this area and we pass close by a butt with a number ten painted on its stone wall, almost immediately crossing a narrow, muddy stream.

8. The path is much more obvious now and has small cairns interspersed along it. About 500 yards after the grouse butt we should arrive at the twin cairns on the summit of Greets Hill (SE 02840 95676).

9. Pass the cairns and we meet a fence, which we should follow to another pair of cairns, situated either side of a gate in the fence.

10. The path now clear and wide, heads downhill past a pile of stones, an old quarry and another large cairn until it meets some more grouse butts.

11. Stay on the obvious track all the way down the hill until we reach a junction of roads with a four-way fingerpost. Turn left here to join the usual route from Grinton and the buildings at Dent's Houses. Now jump to point 6 on page 111.

PART 2 - GRINTON LODGE TO MORLEY'S FOLLY
Approx 4½ miles (7 km) - 2½ to 3 hours

1. With Grinton Lodge at your back, cross the road and follow the bridleway, indicated by the fingerpost, through the heather to another, double fingerpost.

2. At the tarmac road, turn left and follow the road as it climbs steeply up the hill. As the road bends to the left, leave it and pick up a bridleway heading right, marked by a fingerpost (SE 04384 97448). If you wish to follow the short-cut to Dent's Houses, you would stay on the tarmac road (see the section above for a description of this route).

3. We're now on a four-wheel drive track through the heather, which soon becomes a wide green path, easy on the feet. Within ½ a mile of leaving the road, the path drops down to a gate (SE 03838 9723) which we pass through to reach Grovebeck Gill, a shallow stream which we can cross easily by way of the large stones.

4. Beyond the gill the track climbs gently between the heather, soon turning into a wide green path again before coming to a crossroads. A four-wheel drive track crosses our path at right-angles and another track leads almost straight on (slightly right) and this is the path we need to take.

5. This wide four-wheel drive track climbs steadily uphill towards Low Harker Hill. Follow the track uphill for about ¼ of a mile towards two piles of stones on the left side of the path and another on the right that mark the eastern edge of Harker Top (SE 02750 97413).

6. The wide track, now closely skirted by heather on either side, continues over Harker Top to High Harker Hill. Follow the road for another ½ a mile or so to the lonely fingerpost atop an old spoil heap on the wide summit plateau (SE 01648 97185).

7. As the track leaves the summit of High Harker Hill, it describes a neat S; turning right then left, heading downhill all the way.

8. A few moments later the road forks; keep left here, on the main track and head towards a large shooting hut that soon comes into view. This hut may well be unlocked and has chairs and tables enough for a large party. Please leave the hut as you found it, or future walkers may find it locked.

9. Immediately after passing the hut, the road drops down to meet Browna Gill and crosses on a wide plank bridge, before climbing up again to our previous level. Here a large rock offers a seat for two people beside the road, a perfect opportunity to admire the view perhaps.

10. Stay on the main path, ignoring any side tracks that appear and after ¾ of a mile or so keep an eye open for a large pile of stones beside the path on the right.

These are the remains of a very impressive old lime kiln. Although this is now mostly decayed when viewed from the track, it still presents an impressive facade when seen from its base, a short way down the hillside. The size of this kiln suggests that this was no small-scale operation and it would have produced huge quantities of lime to meet the needs of local farmers, who used it as fertilizer and the local mining industry that needed it for mortar for their building work.

---

11. Another couple of hundred yards along the track you will see a cairn off the path to the right (SD 99538 96746). If the weather is clear, this cairn marks a superb viewpoint, from which you can take in the whole of Swaledale. Well worth the short diversion.

12. Even if you don't visit the viewpoint, the cairn is worthy of note, as it forewarns us of a change in direction. Shortly

after passing the viewpoint cairn on your right, look out for a wooden post with an information board on it, beside the path on your left and a narrow track heading off into the heather (SD 99373 96388). This is where we leave the four-wheel drive track for a while.

13. The path through the heather is aided by a cairn, but once you're on it, it's easy to follow. It runs parallel to the track we've just left, for a while at least, but it's easier to join where we did, rather than try to find it later.

The views from here are expansive; down into Swaledale and across to the moors above Reeth and Gunnerside, a fine retrospective on yesterday's walk.

14. The path becomes faint in places but should be easy enough to follow. It soon begins to bend gently left as it enters a narrow valley and you should see a grouse butt on the right, slightly below us. Another one soon appears on the left, a fine stone example topped with a layer of turf. This should have the number two painted on it.

15. The path continues up beside Birks Gill passing butt number three and almost immediately bearing right, crossing the narrow stream above a small waterfall (SD 99233 95806) and climbing up the opposite bank to reach the magnificent butt number four.

16. From here the path pretty much disappears, but as we climb, keep butt number four on the left and follow a ridge of slightly higher ground uphill. This is the right bank of a narrow beck, almost completely submerged and hidden by marsh grass, and easier to hear than see. We keep this beck on our left as we climb gently towards the skyline.

17. Eventually, about 300 yards after crossing the beck you should be able to see a large pile of stones, an old spoil heap ahead of us. Head towards this and we soon reach a clear, wide, stony track (SD 99265 95543).

18. Turn left onto the track as it winds its way gently uphill. Ignore cairns to the left of this wide and obvious track, which we will be following for the next few miles.

200-300 yards along the track, the OS Explorer map (1:25k scale) refers to "Morley's Folly (disused)". A large pile of stones, now mostly grass covered, seems to be the only evidence of a building or structure on this site. One can only presume that the luckless Morley built here while prospecting and nothing ever came of his excavation.

PART 3 - MORLEY'S FOLLY TO CASTLE BOLTON
Approx 4 miles (6 km) - 2 to 2½ hours

1. Almost exactly ½ a mile after joining the track we arrive at a gate in a long fence that cuts directly across the path in front of us (SD 99872 95343). Pass through the gate (the highpoint of today's section) and the track turns left and then right past two large cairns. This is Apedale Head, from where you can appreciate grand views down into the valley and desolate moorland on either side, with the path winding down ahead.

2. The path now passes through a blasted landscape of quarries and spoil heaps but also provides the compensation of glorious views down into Apedale.

3. Continue to descend through the valley, ignoring side tracks off to the left and then the right, stay on the main track, which should be easy to follow even in the worst of conditions.

This valley will forever bear the scars of the lead mining that was carried out here and you pass many spoil heaps, tips, shafts and other remnants of the industry. You will also see many new trees that have been planted along both sides of the valley, to try and return some of the biodiversity to the flora.

4. The road crosses a number of small becks and descends steadily. About 2 miles beyond the gate in point 1, we reach another gate in a fence line cutting across our path (SE 02722 94272). Another 350 yards further on and we reach a staggered crossroads with several buildings and stock pens clustered about it. This is Dent's Houses. The buildings support the sheep pens and the nearby grouse butts.

5. The track coming down the hill on our left is the short-cut over Greets Hill.

6. Turn right (south) before the small stone building with the huge corrugated iron barn attached to it and go through the gate and across the bridge. There are two more buildings on this side of the bridge. The larger of these two buildings is a great place to take shelter from foul weather and it also has a toilet. The building doesn't appear to be locked when not being used, but please leave the room as you found it.

7. Climb the path as it leaves Dent's Houses behind and as it flattens out and undulates across the moorland. The track runs generally straight south though and after ¼ of a mile or so it takes a sharp right (west) turn in front of a gate in a wall (SE 03151 93344). A small stile can be found beside the gate.

8. Leave the road here, saying goodbye to the open moorland, and use the stile to join a green lane that runs between two wire fences.

On the distant skyline to your left you may be able to see the chimney of the Cobscar Smelting Mill and the harsh scar of Redmire Quarry. The buildings and equipment at Cobscar Mill were used for target practice by the army in the early years of the Second World War; the chimney stands some way off at the end of a flue and was spared.

---

9. Follow the green lane downhill, between the fence lines, as it turns right then left before reaching a wide pasture. The fence lines disappear left and right, leaving you looking out over the wide field.

10. The green lane continues almost straight ahead (slightly east of south) to reach the corner of a dry stone wall, which it follows downhill. The path keeps close to the wall, but meanders sometimes to avoid boggy ground, although in wet conditions you may still get wet and muddy boots along this section.

11. After passing a plantation beside the wall, the path moves slightly to the left, becomes a bit more wet and boggy and

reaches a flat concrete bridge over a small stream and then a gate in the dry stone wall at the bottom of the field (SE 03567 92108).

12. Pass through the gate and follow the narrow walled lane as it drops downhill and turns gradually right (west), until it reaches a double fingerpost beside a gate.

13. Ignore the gate and stay on the track as it turns left here, between high hedges and past a residential garden before opening onto the village green in Castle Bolton. Turn right and you will see the impressive remains of Bolton Castle looming high over the village.

CASTLE BOLTON

Castle Bolton has one single dominant feature; its castle, Bolton Castle. The tea room, car park and public toilets that also exist in the village are only there because of the number of visitors that are attracted to the castle. The structure dates back to the 14th century and was the ancestral home (or perhaps fortress would be more appropriate) of the Scrope family. The large village green facing the castle gates is lined with pretty cottages and gives the village an elongated feel.

Car parking is available behind the castle and provided for castle patrons. The fees for car parking are refundable when you pay for entrance into the castle or gardens.

A **telephone box** is located (almost hidden in fact) on the south side of the village green beside a large hedge. The box itself is Grade II listed and dates back to 1935.

There is a **tea room** in the Castle itself. Entry to the majority of the castle is subject to a fee, but the tea room and the **gift shop** are free to enter.

There are **public conveniences** available in the car park, located behind the castle.

A **bus stop** is located beside the castle. Castle Bolton is serviced by bus routes 156 and 157 running between Hawes and Northallerton.

Part 4 - Castle Bolton to Aysgarth
Approx 4 miles (6 km) - 2 to 2½ hours (this does not include any time spent visiting the waterfalls at Aysgarth)

1. After visiting the castle, leave the village on the steep lane heading south, beneath the walls of the castle. Watch out for the dragon! A direct route all the way down the hill on the road will serve our purposes, but if you prefer to avoid the traffic, look out for a drive leaving the road to the right, a couple of hundred yards from the castle (SE 03479 91601). If you follow the road, jump to point 4 below.

2. The drive winds down to a house, where the public Right of Way keeps to the right of the building and passes through the back garden on a slightly sunken paved path down to a narrow green lane and a gate.

3. The lane is a rough path between trees and low walls and is rocky underfoot in places, but after passing through another gate, soon arrives at a road. Turn left along the road for about 250 yards until we arrive at a bus shelter and a road arriving from the left. This is the road from Castle Bolton.

4. Directly opposite this road is a wide gate in the wall on our right and a much narrower wooden gate beside it. Go through the gate, into the field and follow the fence on the left of the field for about 400-500 yards until it reaches another narrow gated stile.

5. In this next field, follow the fingerpost as it guides us half right, across a green path in the middle of the field towards a set of power lines in the right hand corner. Here the path hugs the wall on the left, beneath the power lines for a few yards before a fingerpost directs us left, across the broken wall to a stile just beyond (SE 03697 90567).

6. The stile drops us down to a road, onto which we must turn right, towards the building of Low Thoresby Farm. Keep the farm to our left and follow the path until it becomes a muddy track running between two hedges, this is Thoresby Lane.

> Thoresby Lane and the two fields that follow it are perhaps the muddiest and boggiest section of the whole Way, especially after heavy rain. But they come at the end of the walk and one would hope that the previous 50 miles or so have more than compensated for the possibility of wet and muddy feet at this point.

7. About half way along its length the lane swaps it hedges for dry stone walls, but the underfoot conditions don't improve significantly. Towards the end of the lane, we cross a stream on a wide stone slab and then pass through a wooden gate and a hundred yards later reach the gate at the end.

8. Keep close to the wall on our left through the next field and follow the muddy path past a fingerpost and along to another wide gate, 400-500 yards beyond.

9. The path stays close to the wall on the right in this next field (heading slightly south of west) for about 100 yards until it reaches a fingerpost beside a narrow gated stile (SE 02410 89829). The fingerpost has a small "Footpath" finger, below the main sign for "Castle Bolton" and this indicates the direction we need to take through this large open meadow. There should be a faint green path showing the course of the footpath, as it heads uphill for about 300 yards to a narrow gated stile set high in the wall.

10. Go through this stile and keep left, beside the fence in the next field to reach a gate which gives on to a farm access road. Turn left onto the road and follow it to a red metal gate. The road beyond this gate leads gently downhill to Hollins House. Pass the farmhouse on the left and then look out for a footpath that heads left, off the paved path.

11. The footpath passes through two large vehicle gates and then out into a wide green pasture. The path should be clear across the field as it drops gently for about 300 yards to a smaller gate beside a fingerpost for "Aysgarth Falls" (SE 01974 89011).

12. Go through this gate and keep to the path beside the fence on our right, which we must follow for about 200 yards or so as it bends around to the right. As the fence line

straightens up again it is encroached by a line of short trees coming from the left and we must squeeze between these and the fence. Almost immediately after the trees you should see a faint path heading half left away from the main green path that continues beside the fence. This side path runs down between another line of trees to meet some concrete steps that provide access to the viewing platform at the Lower Falls.

13. When you've visited the Lower Falls, return to the concrete steps and follow them as they join a well laid trail through the woods, several hundred yards to the viewing platform for the Middle Falls. There are plenty of signs along this section and it would be hard to lose your way.

14. The path from the Middle Falls leads to a road. Signposts will take you right, across the road if you want to visit the National Park Centre and their café or turn left along the road to get a view of the Upper Falls as they cascade down beneath Yore Bridge.

15. The road crosses the bridge where we find a tea room on the other side. Stay with the road as it winds steeply up the hill. Views from the bridge and from the right of the road show the High Force of Aysgarth Falls. Follow the road until we reach the Parish Church of St. Andrew on our left.

16. On the opposite side of the road from the entrance to the church you will see a gate set in the wall and a fingerpost pointing us into the field beyond (SE 01108 88464). For the next 500-600 yards we follow a series of narrow pinch stiles through fields and meadows. The path is easy to follow, but should you wish to check your progress, the route runs as follows:

    > Narrow gated stile, steps up to narrow stile, narrow stile, narrow stile, narrow stile, straight ahead past the barn to steps up to narrow stile, past another barn on the right to narrow stile leading into narrow lane.

17. Follow this narrow lane between a hedge on the left and a low wall on the right, for about 100 yards to its end. Turn right through another narrow stile here into a field. Keep

to the left of the field and through another narrow gate, beside a large vehicle gate. We join a road here, lined with houses and we need to follow this as it turns left up the hill. Within 200-300 yards the road enters into Aysgarth village with the green ahead of us.

18. We've arrived at our destination and indeed our origin. The George and Dragon is just to our left and Hamilton's tea room is ahead to our right, both are suitable venues for a celebratory drink.

AYSGARTH

For village facilities in Aysgarth, see page 47.

Walking the Herriot Way

PART 3 - THE MAPS

"I was not able to light on any map or work giving the exact locality of the Castle Dracula, as there are no maps of this country as yet to compare with our own Ordnance Survey maps."

Jonathan Harker, *from Bram Stoker's 'Dracula'*

The maps for this walk are available direct from the website, at no extra charge. Simply use the password provided below to access the special location on the website.

From this page, you will be able to download the maps in PDF format. You can then print the maps and carry them separately from the book, perhaps to be placed in a waterproof map case.

It also ensures you have the latest versions of the maps, with any amendments that may have been made since the book was published.

Webpage: **bit.ly/herriot-way**

Password: **aL81XyEz**

If you have any problems accessing or downloading the maps, please send an email to: **stuart@pocketroutes.co.uk**

OVERVIEW MAP

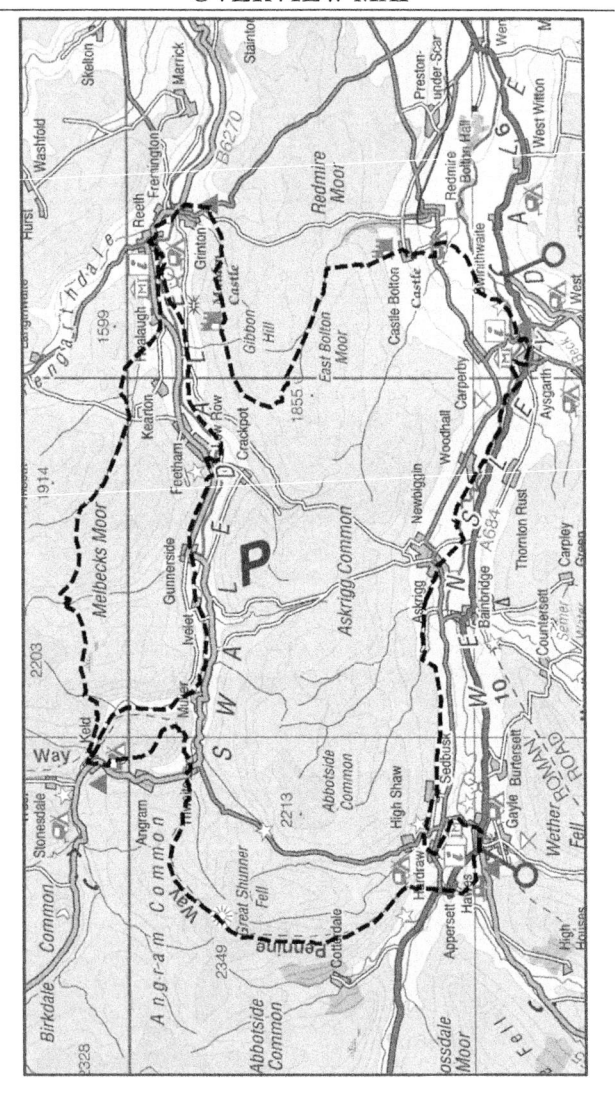

NOTES